BUSINESS FOR LIFE

Build A Profitable Business That Gives You Your Time, Freedom, and Life Back

Jason Wojo, Ph.D.

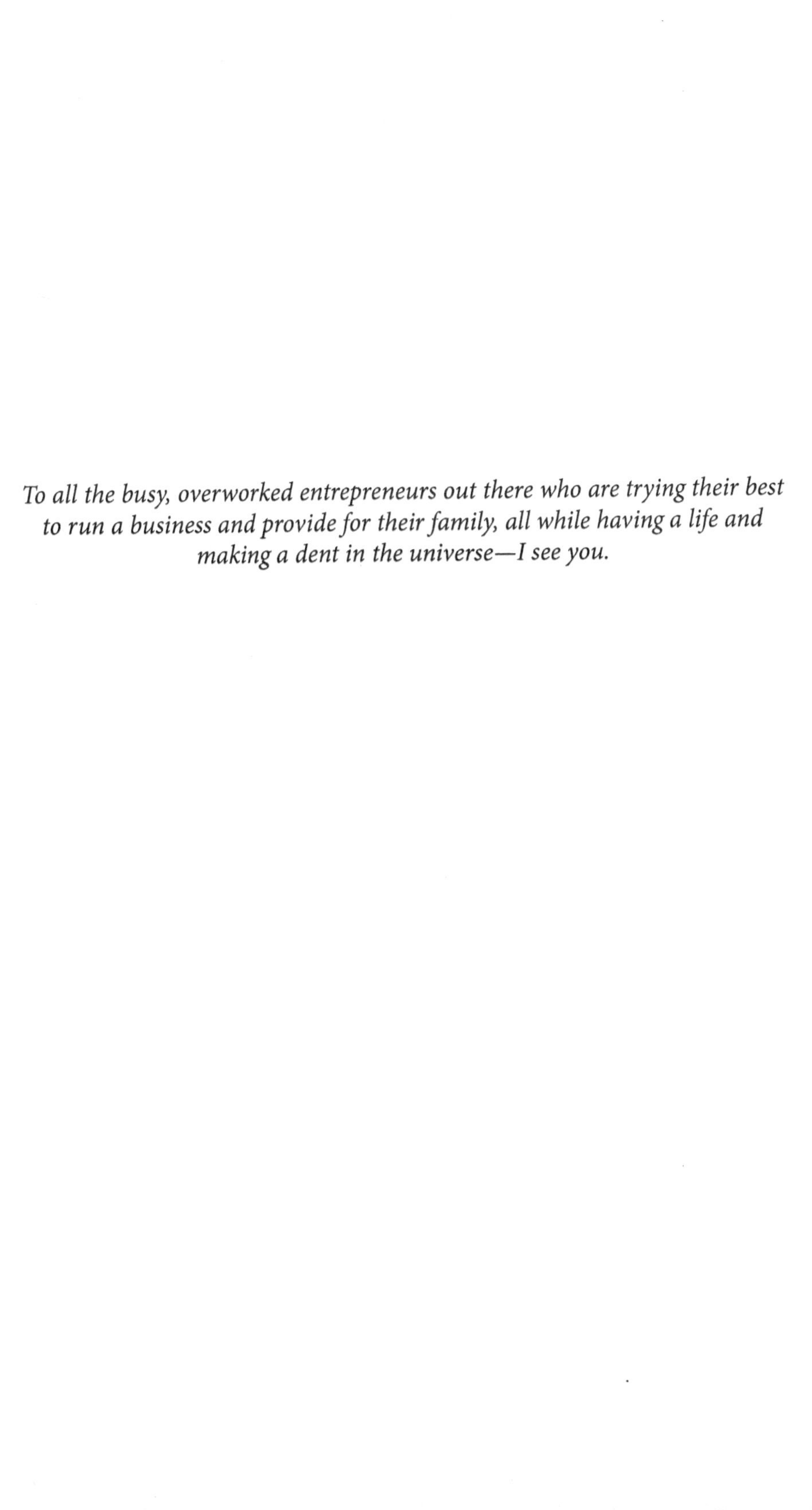

To all the busy, overworked entrepreneurs out there who are trying their best to run a business and provide for their family, all while having a life and making a dent in the universe—I see you.

CONTENTS

PRAISE FOR BUSINESS FOR LIFE

"Business for Life is a must-read for every business owner. The constant struggle of work-life balance seems to always be won by work until you implement the principles of this book. Jason is a genius when it comes to teaching how to develop your vision first and then align your business with the vision so that the business delivers and supports the life you want. I can't wait to see others succeed with the things I've learned directly from Jason over the years."

—Tyler Garns, Founder, Box Out Marketing and Double Your Sales Club

"Business for Life is more than a book - it's a wake-up call for entrepreneurs who've forgotten why they started. Jason Wojo shows us how to reclaim time, vision, and joy while still building real success. His wisdom and methodology have enriched both my business and my life. Every entrepreneur needs this."

—Dobbin Buck, Co-Owner, Chief Revenue Officer, Get You Wired

"Knowing what you want is critical, but it's not enough. In Business for Life, Jason Wojo reveals the concise 4-step framework that has propelled his many students and clients from overworked self-employed workers into fulfilled business owners with companies that truly serve their lives. This book is a MUST READ for any entrepreneur looking to evolve in the new economy and maximize results without working harder."

—Eric Lundberg, Founder, the Aimful companies

"This is the book that finally puts it all together…not just another cautionary tale about getting trapped in your business, but a simple and powerful blueprint to efficiently build (or rebuild) and run your business without it running (or ruining) your life!"

—Heather Greenbaum, Founder, Southern States Vending

"Most entrepreneurs start their business with a dream of freedom, only to end up chained to it, working harder for less peace and joy. In this book, Jason lays out a simple but powerful process that shows you how to reverse that trap. He gives you practical tools to build a business that serves your life, not one that robs you of it. If you've ever felt overwhelmed, overworked, or wondered if owning a business was really worth it, this book is for you."

—Steve Cook, Founder, Lifeonaire

"Most small business owners dream of the day their business can run successfully without them. However, few ever create a plan to make it happen. This book reveals the crucial steps needed to transform your business from a demanding full-time job into a thriving, income-producing machine."

—Joe Turney, Life Coach, Founder, Smalltown Properties

"As a fellow entrepreneur, this book hits uncomfortably close to home, in all the right ways. Business for Life is a step-by-step, real-world process for eliminating chaos, installing systems, and creating a business that can finally run without you. Wojo doesn't just promise freedom; he shows you exactly how to build a business you love without losing the people you love in the process."

—Ben Cope, Founder, Internet Genius Consulting

"Every business owner — or anyone even thinking about starting a business — needs to read this book. Jason captures the entrepreneurial journey so perfectly. Here's how it usually goes… You start with a skill, something people will actually pay for, and the excitement and adrenaline make it all feel easy… until one day, you realize you've built yourself the worst job ever. You feel stuck, lost, and wonder if the only way out is to quit. Jason shows you exactly how to break that pattern and build a business you truly love — one that supports your whole life: your family, friends, customers, and most importantly, yourself. I finished this book feeling completely reinvigorated. It's not just inspiring; it's practical, with a clear blueprint, actionable insights, and steps you can implement right away. I can't recommend Business for Life highly enough. Trust me, your future self will thank you."

—JODY LAYNE, CEO, ACCELERATED MEDICAL PRACTICES

"What I love most about this book is how Jason has decoded the path to freedom and made it simple enough for anyone to apply. As an entrepreneur, I've used the SEAD process across more than a half dozen different businesses, and it consistently delivers results. We've not only freed up our money, but more importantly, over 20 hours a week of our TIME that we now get to spend enjoying life. If you're on the fence, thinking, "I don't have time to read another business book," then you're the exact person this was written for. Grateful to you Wojo."

—SHANNON RICHARDSON, BUSINESS COACH, FOUNDER, SALTY LIFE
PROPERTIES AND PROPERTY MANAGEMENT

FOREWORD

If you've been in business for any length of time, you probably know this feeling: you started your company to gain freedom and control, but somewhere along the way, it started to feel like the business owns you. You work harder than ever, carry the weight of every decision, and keep telling yourself, "Once things slow down, I'll finally take a break." But things never really slow down, do they?

For more than two decades, working with hundreds of thousands of small business owners at Keap (formerly Infusionsoft), I've seen that story play out over and over again. Entrepreneurs with big dreams and even bigger hearts end up buried in the chaos of running their own companies. It doesn't happen because they're undisciplined, unmotivated, or unskilled. It happens because nobody ever showed them how to build a business that *serves* their life instead of *suffocating* it.

That's why this book matters.

Business for Life is a lifeline for entrepreneurs who are tired of being run by their business. It's not another book about grinding harder, hustling more, or scaling just to scale. It's a guide for the driven but overwhelmed entrepreneur who feels stuck on the treadmill, working harder than ever, yet never feeling free. It's for the person who loves their business but wishes it didn't require every ounce of their energy and attention to keep it running. It's for anyone who wants to get back the time, peace, and purpose they've slowly lost to the daily grind.

Jason and I first connected through the Keap community, and from the start, I saw we shared similar values and philosophies. He wasn't chasing growth for ego's sake; he was chasing freedom and fulfillment, both for himself and for the people he serves. That's why our community honored him with Keap's "Let's Grow" Business of the Year Award—a prestigious recognition given to entrepreneurs who use systems and automation to scale with both heart and integrity. Jason didn't win that award for theory; he won it for results. His business was thriving, but so was his life. And that's rare.

Awards and case studies are great, but the reason I agreed to write this foreword is simpler: Jason cares deeply about people. He cares about building businesses and lives worth living. In my experience, that kind of alignment—purpose with performance—is what endures. It's what keeps founders going through the rough patches, what builds teams that believe, and what creates organizations that customers trust. It's also what our Keap community has always stood for: simplifying growth so small businesses can win at work *and* at home.

In this book, Jason hands you the roadmap to do the same. He's not sharing ideas; he's sharing the mechanics of creating time, peace, and fulfillment while still building something profitable and scalable. He'll help you clarify your vision, strip away what doesn't matter, systemize your processes, and build a team that can share the load with you. All so that you can finally experience the freedom you imagined the day you started your company.

As you read, you'll find yourself thinking differently about success. You'll start asking new and better questions. Instead of "How can I get more done?" you'll ask "Is this even worth doing?" Instead of "How can

I make more money?" you'll ask "How can my business better align with and support the life I want?"

That shift—when your business becomes a tool to live the life you want rather than a trap that keeps you stuck—is when everything changes. If you apply what's in this book, you'll not only build a more profitable company, you'll also build margin, peace of mind, and time to enjoy the things that actually matter.

I've spent my career cheering on small business owners—the dreamers, doers, and difference-makers who take risks and make the world better through their work. And I can tell you this: the principles in these pages are the exact ones that will help you keep your passion alive, your priorities straight, and your freedom intact.

Watching Jason live out what he teaches has been inspiring. His commitment to helping others build businesses that serve their lives is evident in everything he does, and *Business for Life* captures that mission perfectly.

So, as you turn the page, don't just read this book—*work* it. Highlight it. Reflect on it. Apply it. Let it challenge the way you think about growth and success. Because if you do, you'll come out on the other side with a business that doesn't just make money, but one that works for you instead of against you.

Here's to building a profitable, purposeful, and peaceful business that gives you your life back.

—Clate Mask Co-founder & former CEO,
Keap (formerly Infusionsoft) Author,
Conquer the Chaos: The 6 Keys to Success for Entrepreneurs

INTRODUCTION

Think back for a moment. Do you remember why you first decided to go into business for yourself? Maybe you were sick of working for "The Man" or dealing with office politics. Maybe you hated someone else controlling your hours, workload, or paycheck. Or maybe you had a skill or passion you wanted to monetize, while getting to be your own boss and having no one to tell you what to do.

Whatever the reason(s) you went out on your own, I'm guessing you also believed owning a business would provide a sense of freedom, financial security, and control of your time. Said differently, it would give you a better life than a job ever could. I mean…that's the point, right? No one starts a business to have *less* freedom, *less* financial security, and *less* control of their life than when they had a nine-to-five. Right?

Funny enough, that's exactly where most business owners end up. Instead of quitting the W-2, cutting back on work, and living the Jimmy Buffett toes-in-the-sand, margarita-in-hand good life, most business owners find themselves working longer and harder, feeling more overwhelmed, stressed, and trapped than they did as employees.

If that's you, you already know the feeling. If you're new to business, here's the picture: work, money, and an ever-growing whack-a-mole to-do list consume your thoughts, time, and attention. Business and its obligations start to spread like cancer into your personal life. You can't take a shower, watch a movie, or go to bed without thinking about work. It feels like you'll never catch up, and life starts to become a blur, like you're on a treadmill that someone is secretly speeding up. Your relationships start to suffer because you're never around, and even in those rare instances when you're physically present, you're distracted and not really there mentally. Arguments with your spouse get more common. You miss your kids' soccer games. And vacations? That's hilarious, yeah right. The only good thing that comes from being too busy is now you have an excuse to skip the gym, which, let's be honest, you hated anyway. Given enough time, the result is burnout, breakdown, and sometimes even bankruptcy. I've seen it. I've lived much of it.

To be fair, not every entrepreneur ends up here. Some have already discovered what I'll share in this book. But in my experience, they are the exception, not the rule. And for every one business owner I see with a business and life they love, I see dozens more that are overwhelmed, struggling, and on the verge of giving up.

So, what's the solution? How can you take back your life without giving up on business success? How can you make the money you want *and* have the time to enjoy it?

That's the focus of this book. The solution is a four-step process I developed called the SEAD process (pronounced *seed*, like one you'd plant in the ground). Each letter stands for a step in the SEAD acronym: **Strategize, Eliminate, Automate, and Delegate.** It's a proven formula to create a business that supports your life rather than sacrifices it. It's a step-by-step operating system for building a life-first business that I've seen work over and over in companies of all different types, sizes, and industries.

My promise is that when you put this process to work and "SEAD your business," you'll gain the time, freedom, and fulfillment you've been chasing. You'll cut back your hours and stop feeling overwhelmed. You'll feel the relief and confidence of having a business that can thrive without you doing all the work. You'll be more focused, effective, profitable, and maybe have fun again. You'll build a *Business for Life*—one you'll never want to retire from because it finally supports the life you want to live. So grab your hat and hold on. You're in for a ride.

WHO THIS BOOK IS FOR

Your time is incredibly valuable, so let's define exactly who will benefit most from this book. (As much as I'd like to think that everyone and their grandmother's cousin would love this, that's probably just not true.)

This book is for entrepreneurs who want a successful business that supports their life instead of consumes it.

You may be the founder, CEO, or hold some other impressive title, and you wear most or all the "hats" in your business. (And if you're honest, you probably design, manufacture, market, sell, and ship the hats too.) You may call yourself a "business owner," but if you're straight with yourself, you're really self-employed, because the whole thing screeches to a halt the moment you're not there.

Still not sure if this is you? Here's a quick quiz. If most of these ten statements feel true, this book was written for you:

1. Your business can't run without you. Every dollar, every task, and every decision depends on you.
2. Despite your best intentions, balls keep getting dropped and projects drag on far too long.

3. You consider a 12-hour workday "part-time" because, hey, there are 24 hours in a day.
4. You don't control your schedule; it controls you.
5. Work stress is eating away at your health, happiness, and peace of mind.
6. People you love keep saying you're never around.
7. Life outside of work has become a blur, and you're missing moments you can't get back.
8. Your house got completely remodeled two years ago, and you just noticed today.
9. You started this business to create freedom—but somewhere along the way, it became a prison.
10. Your org chart looks like the image below.

THE SOLOPRENEUR ORG CHART

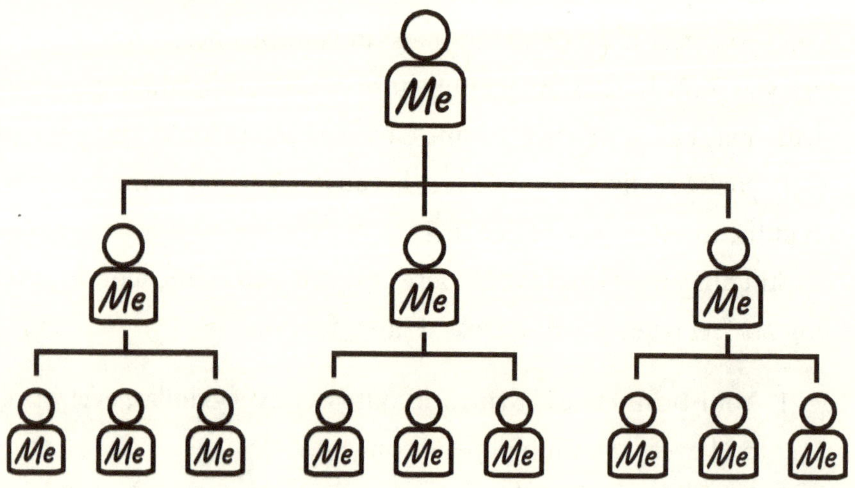

Figure 0.1: A business that completely relies on you has a single point of failure.

If those statements hit a little too close to home…if it felt like I've been shadowing you with a clipboard…then this book is 1,000 percent for you. Reading it can change your life.

In all fairness, here's who won't benefit quite as much from this book:

o Your business already runs smoothly without you. You could vanish for months and it wouldn't skip a beat.

o You work as much or as little as you want, and do it because you choose to, not because you have to.

o You have strong systems, processes, and people in place that keep the business running like clockwork, rain or shine.

So…which group are you? If you're more of the first (no judgment—that was definitely me), then read on. It's going to completely revolutionize how you run your business. If you're in the second group and already have things dialed in, that's awesome. You're living what most business owners dream about. For you, this book may serve more as a tune-up than a transformation.

HOW TO GET THE MOST FROM THIS BOOK

You're a busy business owner with a mountain of things on your plate that were all due yesterday. You don't need another motivational read. You need a system that actually changes how your business runs. This book was designed to be just that: a practical field manual for taking back control of your time, income, and life.

Each section starts with the key reasons why applying this process is a must. This is crucial and will allow you to see the true value of SEAD and what it can do for you. SEAD works, period. I've seen it transform hundreds of businesses and lives. The only variable is whether you execute it. If you read it like entertainment, you'll feel inspired for a few days. If you read it like a playbook, it'll change your life forever.

So before you dive in, make this commitment to yourself:

1. Read with an Application Mindset

Don't race through this just to brag to your buddies that you've read nine books this month. That approach will leave you with only a fraction of the benefit you'd otherwise get if you were to really devour the concepts. Instead, ask yourself, "*Where does this show up in my business?*" and "*What would this look like if I actually implemented it*?" Doing it this way will bridge the gap between knowing and doing.

2. Capture What Matters

As you read, write down action steps and plans for SEADing your business. Underline, highlight, and circle sections that hit you. Capture ideas, thoughts, and golden nuggets. Scribble notes in the margins. By the time you're done reading this book, it should look like your kids and your dog had an unsupervised weekend with it.

This approach will save you lots of time and frustration later. Your notes and highlights will be a cheat sheet as you start applying the concepts, principles, and ideas you've learned.

3. Commit to Moving Forward

Listen, I double pinky swear—what you're about to learn can change everything *if* you choose to apply it. I can say that with confidence because I've taught this process for years and have witnessed countless businesses and lives reinvented. I know without a doubt that you can be next, but you have to commit to taking action.

To help you along your journey, I've made available several powerful resources on BusinessForLife.com. You can also message me there. Tell me why this shift is a *must* for you and why failure isn't an option. I read and respond to all messages personally (albeit sometimes slowly), and I'll be in the front row cheering for you, my fellow life-first entrepreneur.

WHAT TO EXPECT

Before we begin, let's get a lay of the land so you can use this book most effectively. While you can certainly jump to the specific chapters that interest you most, I'd recommend not skipping the early foundational sections. Even though you might be eager to learn how to eliminate, automate, or delegate, the first chapters will help you grasp the true importance of building a Business for Life.

In **Part I,** we'll challenge the deeply ingrained belief that success means working more and sacrificing your life. You'll explore why so many entrepreneurs feel trapped by their businesses and uncover the real reasons behind overworking, burnout, and the loss of freedom. Most importantly, you'll redefine the true purpose of business: to support the life you want to live.

In **Part II** you'll be introduced to the philosophy and necessity behind the SEAD process. Through powerful examples and reframes, you'll see and appreciate the difference between owning a business and operating a job. This section shows why SEAD isn't just helpful, but essential for lasting freedom, stability, and fulfillment.

In **Part III** we begin with the "S" step of SEAD: Strategize. You'll learn how to define a clear vision for your ideal life and intentionally design your business to complement that life, rather than compete with it. You'll gain clarity on what you should be doing in the business, how much you should be working, and how to set up your business with a life-first approach.

In **Part IV**, we move into the "E" step: Elimination. This step is about simplifying and streamlining your business by removing everything that doesn't serve a valuable purpose. You'll learn how to identify unnecessary tasks, distractions, and complexity that drain your time, energy, and resources. By cutting clutter and creating space, you and your team can move faster and focus on what matters most.

Part V will open your eyes to the game-changing power of "A"; Automation. You'll discover the vast possibilities of tasks that technology can fulfill, allowing you to reclaim your time and reduce mental load. This section reveals how to leverage automation to scale, create consistency, and free up manual bandwidth.

In **Part VI** we put a bow on the SEAD process. You'll see how this section walks you through the mindset, systems, and practical steps to successfully find, hire, train, and lead a team. You'll learn how to build a winning team and solid structure that allows your business to thrive without you being involved at every turn.

In **Part VII** we tie the entire SEAD process together into a simple, sustainable way of running your business. You'll see how the four steps work together as an ongoing operating system to create the life and business you desire, complete with time and financial freedom, fun, and a sense of fulfillment.

Lastly, **Part VIII** helps you move from insight to action. It's a bridge from reading the book to living the results it promises. I share practical next steps, additional resources, and support to help you continue building your very own Business for Life.

PART I
THE FOUNDATION FOR FREEDOM

"There is only one success: to be able to spend your life in your own way."

—CHRISTOPHER MORLEY

grew up thinking the key to a great life was having a great job. Something well-paying, with an impressive title, and a corner office. Business wasn't even on my radar. My parents were both W-2 employees, so that's the path I learned. I vividly remember a conversation with my dad as I neared high school graduation. On the topic of my options, he said, "Well, you can either go get a minimum wage job…or go to college, then get a higher paying job." *Okay then, college it was.* But because I didn't want just a good life—I wanted a great one—I decided that more education was the ticket.

Fifteen years later (*yes, fifteen*), I emerged with two bachelor's degrees, a master's, and a PhD. I was finally ready to take on the world and start living the dream. I got my very first job working in Washington, D.C. and it checked all the boxes for a good job. But only a few short weeks into the position, it hit me like a splash of cold water—I had made a huge mistake. I realized I couldn't work for someone else.

The problem wasn't the job, my coworkers, or my boss. What made it unbearable was the thought of someone else controlling that much of my life. Someone else calling the shots on when I worked, how much I worked, what I worked on, who I worked with, and how much I earned. It all made me sick. I wanted the freedom to do what I wanted, earn the money I deserved, and design my future on my own terms.

What did I do? After months of soul-searching, sleepless nights, and agonizing that I'd wasted fifteen years of my life, the answer became painfully clear: I had to start my own business and become my own boss.

Terrified, lost, and not knowing the first thing about business, I chose real estate investing. I'd seen a few episodes of HGTV's Flip This House and thought, Hmm… this doesn't look too hard. (Spoiler alert: TV does not reflect reality.)

I learned everything I could and jumped in headfirst. From day one it was chaotic, busy, and stressful, but I chalked it up to my inexperience. Once I figured things out, I told myself, it would get easier.

Time passed and I got better. I gained confidence and experience. I even started making real money. But nothing actually changed. I was still buried, stressed, and working way more than I wanted.

I felt just as out of control as when I had a job. In many ways, even more so. I traded working forty hours a week in my W-2 to sixty-plus for myself. I substituted one boss for a worse one (myself), who violated every labor law known. I lived in a constant state of stress and overwhelm. On paper I owned a business, but in reality, it owned me. And no matter how hard I worked, things never seemed to get better or slow down. My dream of freedom had turned into a nightmare.

I kept pushing and pushing until everything eventually came to a grinding halt. I went through a painful divorce, sank into a deep depression, and stayed in bed for weeks. And guess what? When your business relies entirely on you, the moment you stop, the income stops too. I hit rock bottom, and to stretch my last bit of money, I had to move into one of my investment properties, sleeping on an air mattress in a back bedroom while the house was being renovated.

My options were clear: throw in the towel and go back to a job, or reinvent myself and my business, the right way.

CHAPTER 1:
FROM LAB COAT TO LIFE-FIRST BUSINESS

realized that if I wanted a different outcome, I had to start doing things differently. After racking my brain on how I could create a business that didn't own me, it hit me. I already had the tools to figure it out. See, that decade-and-a-half education taught me two extremely valuable things: how to learn, and how to think like a scientist. I could analyze data, form hypotheses, design experiments, and solve problems methodically. I'd just never thought of taking that approach out of the lab and into the world of business. It was a forehead-slapping, "duh" moment for sure.

The problem I set out to solve was simple: *how do I build a business I love? One that wasn't built on my back and would destroy my life. One that I never want to retire from and that gives me both freedom and fulfillment.* In short, a *Business for Life.*

I went to work like a mad scientist, experimenting in my own businesses and studying other business owners. I compared those trapped by their work with those living freely. I teased out the differences, pieced together the puzzle, and started to see patterns emerge.

I saw that the most successful business owners (successful using my definition) started with a vision. They intentionally put life over work and built businesses that aligned with that life. Their vision shaped what their businesses looked like. This became the **Strategize (S)** step of the SEAD process.

Next, I noticed the best businesses were lean and simple. Most weren't monstrous organizations with bloated org charts. Complexity was kept to a minimum, and there weren't lots of wasted resources. They stayed focused and cut everything that didn't move them forward. Seeing this and replicating it in my own businesses, **Eliminate (E)** became the next addition to the SEAD process.

As I continued, I discovered the incredible power of tools, systems, and technology. I found that automation could reduce mistakes and free up people to focus on the important work. Every time I automated, I gained hours and consistency. This became **Automate (A)**.

And lastly, I gained a deep appreciation of having strong teams. I experienced the value of building trust, empowering team members, and fostering a culture of performance, results, and accountability. The more I delegated, the faster we grew. You guessed it, **Delegate (D)** completed the SEAD process.

THE FOUR STEPS OF THE SEAD PROCESS

Figure 1.1: *The SEAD process is a simple, step-by-step approach to free you from the shackles of business busyness.*

This may all sound simple, obvious, and straightforward, but SEAD was not born in a single moment of brilliance. It was developed through years of testing, failing, and refining. Piece by piece, the formula took shape, and the results, both in my own businesses and in hundreds of others, have been nothing short of remarkable.

To be clear, the concepts of elimination, automation, and delegation aren't new or unique, and I'm not the first to talk about them. Others have discussed them before me with varying degrees of clarity, depth, and novelty. But what you now hold in your hands is a proven, reliable framework to reclaim your life without sacrificing business success. Using SEAD, I and many others have cut hours and stress, increased income, rediscovered the joy of business, and most importantly, experienced the freedom that business *should* provide.

THE LIE THAT COSTS ENTREPRENEURS THEIR LIVES

There's an incredibly damaging belief held by entrepreneurs that almost guarantees you'll sacrifice your life and build a business you resent. It's the idea that money is the ultimate scorecard of success.

Yes, money matters. It's the oxygen your business needs to survive. But if your business is thriving financially while your life is falling apart, that's not success. What good is money if you're too stressed, busy, or exhausted to enjoy it? What good is income if you hate the work it takes to generate it? Money is not the purpose of business. **The purpose of business is to give you the life you want.**

Please read that sentence again. Memorize it, stick it on your refrigerator, and hang it over your bed. Even better, consider getting a full-color tattoo of it somewhere highly visible as a constant reminder. It's that important, because this single belief dictates how you build and run your business.

If that sounds naïve, foolish, or unrealistic, let me assure you, it's not. Truth be told, it's the only way to stay in business long-term. Otherwise, at some point you'll likely close your doors due to a head-on collision between your personal life and work.

What does a life-first business look like? At a high level, it gives you:

- **Time freedom and flexibility.** You work as much or as little as you choose, and enjoy your life, whether that's traveling, spending time with loved ones, taking afternoon naps (a personal favorite), or just having time for yourself.

- **Financial support.** You should be able to fully fund your desired lifestyle, without stressing over bills or penny-pinching.
- **Purpose and meaning.** Your business should be fun, fulfilling, and a productive outlet for your skills, interests, and values.

Said another way, your business should support your life, not sacrifice it.

CHAPTER 2:
THE REAL REASONS YOU CAN'T STOP WORKING

Before we dive into the SEAD process, it's important we pause for a moment. The reason being, if you really want to work less in the future, you first need to understand *why* you're working so much now. You might be thinking, "*Uh, isn't it obvious? I have too many things to do! You really have a PhD?!*" Fair enough, but stay with me.

I'd urge you to consider that this is only partially true, and that the sheer number of tasks on your plate probably isn't the only reason you're grinding out all those long hours. There's a very high chance that other reasons are also driving your behavior, even if you're not aware of them.

The reason we cover these is because even if you SEAD your business, you'll continue to overwork unless you deal with those hidden drivers. You'll just have a bigger, more "efficient" version of the same problem. That's why, in this section, we're going to look at what *really* keeps business owners chained to their work.

How do you know whether you might have an issue? Here's the tough-love truth: **If you're always busy and constantly running around with your hair on fire, something is wrong.**

Along these lines, it's important to realize that busyness isn't the problem—it's a symptom of an underlying problem. Just like having a stuffy nose and body aches are symptoms of an infection, constant busyness points to something else happening under the hood. Yes, there are unavoidable busy seasons within both life and business. That's normal. But if there's *never* a break, if you're *never* able to step back and breathe, and if you're constantly redlining the engine, then you need to admit something's off and needs to be addressed.

From talking with and working alongside hundreds of business owners, I've found two main reasons they struggle to peel themselves away from their business. The first is a lack of the required skills to do so, (not knowing how to eliminate, automate, or delegate effectively. Don't worry, we'll cover that.)

The second reason is mindset: the beliefs or fears that make you feel guilty, lazy, or anxious when you step back from work. These inner roadblocks keep you chained to your business and prevent you from embracing the concept of working less.

THE ROADBLOCKS TO STEPPING BACK

Entrepreneurship is a difficult beast to tame. It takes a delicate balance of big-picture, strategic thinking and front-line tactical execution, a combination of hope and optimism, tempered by pragmatism and realism, and the merger of the creative and analytical. It also demands perseverance, boldness, and courage. It's a tall order for sure, and to add a cherry on top, all of that still isn't enough. *I know, super encouraging, right?*

To truly thrive, you need more than just skills. You need the right mindset. Your beliefs about work will dictate whether your business supports your life or strangles it. Sadly, many entrepreneurs believe nonstop work is normal. It's not. It's a direct path to burnout and resentment.

Do you have mental hangups that prevent you from taking your foot off the gas? Limiting beliefs that affect how you approach work/life balance? Let's find out. Finish this sentence with the first thing that comes to mind: *If I'm not working all the time, then…"* Don't overthink it. Go with your first honest answer.

Common answers include the following: *"I'm lazy." "I'd feel guilty." "I'm leaving money on the table." "I'm wasting my abilities." "People will think I'm failing." "My competition will pass me." "I'd be bored." "I'll have to face what I've been avoiding."* Or *"I'm letting people down."*

Now, maybe none of those came up for you. Maybe you pictured yourself reclining on a beach sipping a mojito. If so, sweet…save me a spot.

But for most business owners, that's not the case. A host of beliefs and fears keep them chained to their business. And unless they're addressed, the odds of stepping out of your business are about as slim as outrunning a pack of wolves with a steak strapped to your back.

See, even if you build a business that can run without you, if you don't do the mental work, nothing changes. You'll just find new ways to stay busy. Maybe you'll scale, or maybe you'll spend time extinguishing mysterious fires in the business that continue to ignite, not realizing you're the arsonist, trying to find ways to keep yourself busy.

Freedom shows up in your mind before it shows up on your calendar. Only after you're mentally and emotionally comfortable with the idea of working less can you move on to the *how.* So before we go there, let's unpack the most common mental roadblocks business owners face and how to overcome them.

Roadblock #1: The Grind Mentality

Our culture glorifies being busy. We proudly display our "badge of busy" like a medal of honor, as my friend Dobbin Buck likes to say. Phrases like "rise and grind" echo through the business world with bravado.

This mentality feeds heavily on motivational hype. It's like an adrenaline-pumping halftime pep talk when you're down by two touchdowns in the championship game. You get fired up to push harder, do whatever it takes, and fight to the death. And in the short term, it works. You go into battle, win the day, and come home exhausted yet proud.

Sounds epic, right? But there's a problem: over time, this becomes a death sentence for life outside of work. Glorify the grind long enough, and you'll end up sacrificing everything on its altar. I don't know anyone who has successfully maintained this approach for any sustained length of time without burning out or blowing up their health, relationships, or happiness. In short bursts? Sure, hustle has its place. But stretched out over years, it's not a strategy—it's a slow-motion car wreck.

There is one exception I want to address. If you've created your vision for the life you want, and all you *truly* want to do is work (and you're fine with the consequences), then more power to you. Go for it. Who am I to say that's wrong? But if you want to have both a full life *and* successful business, this isn't the way, even if you absolutely love working. It's like candy. I love Almond Joy bars. But if that's all I eat, there will be not-so-good consequences. Long-term, constant hustle works the same way.

A close cousin to the grind mindset that's worth mentioning is the belief that *more is better,* or *bigger is better*. More deals. Higher revenue. A larger team. While there's nothing inherently wrong with any of those and I love aspirations, be sure it's not your ego driving the bus. Here's the truth: More isn't better. Bigger isn't better. *Better* is better. And how do you define *better*? By how closely it matches your vision. Not by what impresses others or what you think you're "supposed" to strive toward.

Roadblock #2: Work Becomes Your Identity

My guess is you're pretty good at business and making money. (*Not yet? Don't sweat it. Being good at business is a skillset you can absolutely learn.*) And it feels good to be good at things, right? I mean, who doesn't like the feeling of competence and accomplishment? And along with that mastery comes praise, financial success, and recognition. You're rewarded both *externally*, through others' affirmation, and through tangible results like more money. You're rewarded *internally* with an intoxicating sense of pride and satisfaction. It's a double-whammy and the most basic form of positive reinforcement.

But there's a danger here too. If you build your identity around your ability to produce results in your business, you'll never want to step back. This risk is greater if your needs for praise and recognition aren't being met outside of work. Maybe your spouse doesn't show appreciation. Maybe your kids just see you as the chef, taxi driver, and ATM. Or maybe your friends still treat you like the same person they knew decades ago, complete with jokes about the bowl haircut you had when you were twelve.

When this happens, work becomes your main source of affirmation, so you double down and work more. You spend less and less time outside of work, further reducing outside sources of connection, worth, and recognition. It becomes a downward spiral, and at some point, it's difficult to recover. You've alienated your friends and family, you don't have any hobbies, you're 40 pounds overweight, and your mental and emotional health are in the gutter. I've seen this happen more than I care to admit.

Here's what you've got to realize: you are not your job. You are not your business. You're not your skills, abilities, awards, or accolades. Your self-worth isn't your net worth. You are more than what you produce. We live in a culture that idolizes work-based success, but that's not the game you want to play if you want a full, meaningful life. You need areas outside of work where you feel valued, alive, and connected. Otherwise, you'll keep pouring yourself into business, until it all collapses.

Roadblock #3: But What Will Others Think?

Even if you're desperate to work less and are feeling the crushing weight of the grind, there may be a quiet voice inside holding you back that says: *"But what will my clients think? My investors? My competitors? Won't they see me as lazy or uncommitted?"*

This fear is real, and it keeps many entrepreneurs trapped working long hours; not because the business needs it, but because they're afraid of how it *looks* if they don't.

The truth is, **no one is paying attention to how much you work. They pay attention to your results.** Your clients don't care if you worked twenty hours last week or eighty. They only care that you solved their problem. Your investors don't care if you pulled an all-nighter. They're looking at growth metrics. Your competitors are trying to beat you in the market, not win a hustle contest.

In fact, some of the most respected entrepreneurs in the world are known for working *less*, not more:

- **Warren Buffett** spends 80% of his day reading and thinking—not in meetings or running the company.
- **Tim Ferriss** built his brand on the 4-Hour Workweek and is taken seriously across industries.
- **Sara Blakely** (Spanx founder, billionaire) has openly talked about prioritizing time with her kids over endless work hours.

The business world respects *effectiveness*, not exhaustion. If your business is thriving, your clients are happy, and your revenue is strong, no one questions how many hours you logged. They might even assume you're a genius for getting better results in less time. The question you should be asking isn't "*What will others think?*" but rather, "*Why do I care more about appearing busy than actually being free?*"

Roadblock #4: "I'm Doing It for My Family"

This one might ruffle some feathers, but it still needs to be said. You've probably heard (or used) the phrase, "I'm doing it for my family," as a way to justify overworking. I used to say it too. And if you'd challenged me back then on its truthfulness, we would have drawn pistols for a duel at high noon. But looking back, I can admit that I was lying to myself.

Of course I wanted to provide for my family, but if I'm honest, there was a hefty dose of ego in the mix too. I had a chip on my shoulder, and wanted to prove to both myself and others that I could do it. I wanted the recognition and praise that came with success, and I used my family as a noble justification for chasing it.

If I'd really been doing it for them, I would have given them what they wanted most—my time and attention. But if you'd looked at my calendar back then and where I spent my time, you'd see that work was in the front seat and my family was riding in the trunk.

That realization was a painful pill to swallow. I felt ashamed that I hadn't seen the truth earlier and felt devastated by how my misplaced priorities hurt my family.

Now to be clear, I'm not saying you should stop working altogether or spend every waking moment with your family. I'm also not saying that providing for your family isn't admirable. It absolutely is. But once your basic financial needs are met, ask yourself what your family values more: the bigger house and newer cars, or *more of you*? They might gladly trade some of the "stuff" for more of your time, attention, and presence. And if you're not sure what they want, just ask them. Then make sure your actions match what they tell you.

While we're at it, let's hit a related idea: "I want to give my kids all the things I never had." While it's a nice thought, the problem is that it's often taken too far and ends up backfiring. Kids who get everything often don't learn to appreciate work or understand the value of money. You've probably encountered these kids, either while still young or as grown adults, and my guess is your impression of them isn't very favorable. They're often lazy, entitled, and arrogant. Said differently, despite your best intentions, you may be hurting your kids. When you give them whatever they want and cater to their every wish, you stunt their growth and ability to thrive. You're stealing their initiative and resourcefulness and robbing them of a sense of value, purpose, and accomplishment. Rather, consider the approach that the famous martial artist Bruce Lee once recommended: "Instead of buying your children all the things you never had, you should teach them all the things you were never taught."

Roadblock #5: The "What Ifs"

Another big reason many entrepreneurs overwork is what I call the "what-ifs." What if the market shifts? What if my competitors catch up? What if the economy slows down? What if that new law passes? What if…what if…what if?

Fear whispers (or screams) endless doomsday scenarios, and in response we attempt to outwork our worries. We dig moats around our business, hoping to keep uncertainty out.

But here's the reality: if you tried to plan for every possible thing that could go wrong, you'd never even get out of bed in the morning. *Everything* is uncertain in life and business. Always has been, and always will be. And while it's smart to prepare for what's likely, you can't let fear run your decision-making process.

The only "what if" worth fearing is this: *What if nothing changes?* What if one year, five years, or ten years from now, you're still stuck right where you are today?

Roadblock #6: Fear of Extra Time

It might surprise you, but many entrepreneurs dislike—or are even afraid of—free time. They see non-work activities as unproductive or wasteful and secretly resent anything that pulls them away from work. Look a little closer though, and you'll often find fear hiding underneath.

Some are afraid they'll relax and never get their hunger back. Others fear losing their edge or breaking momentum. Some worry they don't have any passions and that life would be boring. And still others fear becoming "average," imagining themselves spending days on end plopped on the couch, binge-watching the latest season of *Dance Moms* with a bag of chips.

Free time can also force people to face things they'd rather avoid— marriage struggles, health issues, money stress, or past trauma. Work becomes a convenient escape and a way to bury your head in the sand. You keep your hands busy and your mind distracted. Of course, this approach usually makes things worse, but in the short term, staying busy feels like relief.

I coached a successful business owner who was very well-known in her industry. She made a great income, but frequently worked 70-80 hours a week. She told me she wanted to date, but said her schedule made it impossible. Together we built a plan to cut her hours in half, and she was beyond excited. But weeks later, nothing had changed. After a heart-to-heart conversation, she finally admitted she was afraid of having free time because it meant she'd have to face the possibility of rejection. She'd had a very painful breakup years prior, and so her relentless work schedule wasn't about productivity at all. It was a protective mechanism to keep her from getting hurt again.

Roadblock #7: No Vision

The last reason we'll discuss for why entrepreneurs overwork isn't related to mindset at all. It's the lack of a life vision. We'll go deeper into this later, but it's important to mention here because it's one of the main reasons business owners don't step away from work.

Among other things, your vision includes the activities, relationships, and experiences that matter most to you. Without it, work will become the default because you'll have nothing else intentionally planned to fill your time. After all, if you don't have any meaningful interests outside of work, it makes sense to keep working. It beats sitting around bored, right? That's why having a clear vision matters so much. When your vision and calendar are full of things that excite you, it creates bookends for when and how much you work.

A few years back, I was hired to coach a wealthy business owner. He was desperate to regain a sense of joy and meaning in his life. For years, all he did was work. He prided himself on being first into the office and the last to leave. Evenings, weekends, holidays…he worked them all. But over time, this approach took a heavy toll. He lost all his non-work friends, was on his third divorce, his kids hated him, and he couldn't name a single hobby or activity he enjoyed. He actually had to think back to his childhood to even remember what fun felt like. Without a vision, his life had narrowed to nothing but work, and it was costing him everything else that mattered.

What Do You Think?

Do any of these reasons for overworking feel relevant to you? Did any hit home or touch a nerve? Don't brush that feeling off. It's important to face anything that surfaced, because in order to step away from the grind, you'll need to identify and overcome the roadblocks that keep you busy.

KEY TAKEAWAYS

1. The Biggest Purpose of Your Business Is to Give You the Life You Want

This central truth must guide every decision in your business. You didn't get into business to make your life worse. You should love your business, and it should deliver time freedom, financial stability, and fulfillment.

2. Having a Vision Is Critical to Your Success

A clear life vision is the guiding document that represents your ideal life in all areas. It acts as both a blueprint and a compass, ensuring your business decisions align with your personal goals and values, while stopping work from taking over your life.

3. Your Business Must Be Set Up Correctly

Many business owners stay stuck as the hub of their business and never evolve from being self-employed. This leads to overwhelm, exhaustion, and the constant feeling that you can never catch up. Until your business can run without you doing everything, it will own you.

4. The SEAD Process Is Your Roadmap to Freedom

SEAD (Strategize, Eliminate, Automate, and Delegate) is a four-step process designed to free business owners from the chaos of being "stuck in everything." It gives you a systematic way to strip away what doesn't matter, simplify what does, and shift responsibilities off your plate so that your business complements your life instead of consuming it.

5. Overworking Isn't Just About Your To-Do List

Long hours aren't only about workload. They often stem from subconscious fears, misplaced identity, societal pressure, and a lack of clarity about what truly matters. When you uncover why you work so much, you'll break free from the shackles of endless hustle.

PART II

THE CASE FOR SEAD

"If your business depends on you, you don't own a business — you own a job."

— MICHAEL E. GERBER

Many years ago, I came across a well-known parable called The Mexican Fisherman, and it had a major impact on me. It's an enlightening tale about ambition, goals, and life.

The first time I read it, I felt like I'd been punched in the gut. I realized that I was the American businessman in the story. I was trying to build an empire, and it was consuming every part of my life. I was either working, thinking about work, or sleeping as little as possible just so I could get back to work. And for what? To live a "better" life? In reality, I was ruining my life in pursuit of it. The things that mattered most didn't even require the money I was killing myself to make.

That lesson stayed with me. But years later, I began to see the parable differently. I started to view the story through the lens of a business owner, not just an operator. But before I share my revised version, let me share a paraphrased version of the original for context:

An American businessman, burned out and breaking down from long hours and work stress, was ordered by his doctor to take a vacation in a quiet Mexican village to regain his health. One morning, while pacing the beach with his mind racing about work, he spotted a fisherman on the pier. He approached the fisherman and complimented him on his catch.

"Nice fish," the American said. "How long did it take you to catch them?"

"Only a little while," replied the fisherman.

Puzzled, the American asked, "Why not stay out longer and catch more?"

The fisherman shrugged. "This is enough to feed my family and still have leftovers for my friends." he replied.

"But what will you do with the rest of your day?"

"I'll go home, play with my children, take a nap with my wife in the afternoon, and in the evening, I'll stroll into town for a cerveza and to play guitar with my friends. My life is full, señor," he said with a content smile.

The American scoffed, "You're doing it all wrong! If you worked longer, you could catch more fish, sell them, and buy a boat. Keep catching fish, selling them, and reinvesting, and over time, you could have a whole fleet and dozens or even hundreds of workers. Done right you could build a fishing empire, and in twenty years, you'd be a rich man!"

"Rich?" the fisherman asked. "And then what?"

The American beamed. "That's the beauty of it! You could do whatever you want. You could fish for a little in the mornings, go home and play with your children and nap with your wife in the afternoons, and go into town in the evenings to enjoy a beer and play music with your friends."

Most people stop at the irony. The fisherman was already living the life the American suggested he sacrifice to build an empire, only to return to it decades later. Not only that, but the advice the American gave was exactly what landed him burned out in the doctor's office to begin with.

But years later, I realized there was another layer hiding underneath. The fisherman's peaceful life has a fatal flaw. Let's continue the story and find out what it is.

The American leaves, and life continues for the fisherman as normal. Then one day, he wakes up with a fever. His body aches and he can barely stand. For three days, he stays in bed. For three days, no fish. And for three days, no income.

As he lies there, his mind starts to wander: *What if I'm sick for a couple of weeks? Or a month? How will my family eat? What if it was my wife or child that got sick instead? I'd be trapped between being there for someone I love or keeping my family fed.* The thoughts didn't stop there: *What if I wanted to travel? What if I just got tired of fishing?*

The questions revealed something uncomfortable: his peaceful life is held together by a single fragile thread—him.

When he recovers, he decides to do something small but significant. He takes his extra fish, sells them at the market, and uses that money to pay someone else to fish with him.

At first, it's only enough for a couple hours. But then he sells those fish too, and before long, he has enough to pay for a full day's work. Then he hires another fisherman. Then another. Eventually he starts going out only when he wants to. His afternoons and evenings are still full of family, naps, and music, but now they're backed by a foundation that continues whether he's on the pier or not.

See the difference? The fisherman didn't build an empire. He didn't sacrifice his life for decades. He just made one small shift: he stopped being the single point of failure. Let's create that same freedom and flexibility for you, using SEAD to provide the foundation.

CHAPTER 3:
WHAT HAPPENS WHEN YOU SEAD YOUR BUSINESS

As I was developing the SEAD process and looking for an easy-to-remember acronym, I landed on SEAD because it mirrors the incredible power of a seed in nature. A single, tiny seed, once planted and nurtured, will take root, grow, and eventually produce a harvest. It's pretty remarkable when you stop and think about it.

The same thing happens once you use the SEAD process in your business. With time and consistency, you'll produce a harvest of your own: a profitable, self-sustaining entity that supports the life you want to live. You'll build strong roots that support your business during slow seasons, downturns, or unexpected challenges, and set the foundation for future growth. It will produce results no matter what industry you're in, how long you've been operating, or how much experience you have. Whether you're a real estate investor, pizza shop owner, or foreign language school, SEAD gives you the proven framework to strengthen your business and design a life you love.

To hit this home and show you why implementing this is a game changer, let's look at the benefits of SEAD. Here are some of the biggest ways SEAD can transform your business and life:

SEAD Benefit #1: Improve Your Chances of Success

The stats on business failure are pretty discouraging. According to the U.S. Bureau of Labor Statistics, about half of all new businesses fail within five years, 65% by year 10, and only 25% are left standing after 15 years.[1] Put simply, three out of four businesses don't make it. Ouch. Based on those stats, you'd be better off playing blackjack in Vegas.

Here's where it gets interesting though. We can all understand *early* business failure, right? You're still learning the ropes, making mistakes, and figuring it out. But why do businesses continue to fail years down the road? From what I've seen, a major contributor is holding on to an owner-centric business design for far too long. You either plateau, get overwhelmed, burn out, or, if by some chance the business does does actually grow, it actually just acclerates the splat.

The irony of this situation (and what catches many well-meaning entrepreneurs) is that what was required for success in the beginning, will sabotage you later. When you first started, it was probably just you, a dream, and a lot of hard work. You were doing everything from A-to-Z yourself: you were in the field, in the back office, and on the roof. That's normal and how most businesses get off the ground. But at some point, unless you release control and add systems, tools, and people, you'll plateau or even backslide. Your plate starts looking like one of those heaping bowls at a Mongolian grill, packed to the limit of where gravity and friction meet, and what used to be manageable now becomes crushing.

---

1   https://www.bls.gov/bdm/us_age_naics_00_table7.txt

At this tipping point, most owners try one of three fixes:

1. **Work more hours.** You try to double down and cover the extra responsibilities yourself. After all, you're the rockstar who started this whole thing, right? This approach is admirable, but it's usually fruitless. You're trying to fix a long-term problem with a short-term solution. This only speeds up the burnout because you're speeding up the treadmill, not slowing it down.

2. **Hire help in a panic.** While a step in the right direction, the problem here is that it's too late. You've waited too long and so you're desperate. You rush the hire, skimp on the training, and provide no leadership, which guarantees disaster.

3. **Quit.** Either the business implodes due to dropped balls, missed opportunities, and a deteriorating reputation, or the owner decides the stress, lost time with family, and headaches just aren't worth it anymore.

You may be wondering if having an owner-centric business model is really that much of a problem, so let's look at a few of the commonly cited reasons for business failure: having a bad model, weak marketing, and poor leadership. If you look deeper, you'll see they're all symptoms of not enough focused time in those areas (whether in learning or execution). When you're doing everything yourself, you're not able to give attention where it's needed.

This might sound oversimplified, so take a look for yourself:

- **Bad business model?** It's because you didn't have the time or knowledge to run the numbers, think through all the angles, and design a better one.
- **Weak marketing?** You haven't done enough research on your ideal customer or developed the copywriting skills to connect

with them. The solution? Yep—having more focused time to learn and test.

- **Poor leadership?** You already know the fix. More quality time devoted to becoming a leader people want to follow.

And I need to say it one more time: working longer hours won't solve long-term issues. It only compounds the problems. It's like a cortisone shot for a bum shoulder. It may provide short-term relief, but it doesn't *fix* anything, and over time just causes more damage.

That's why adopting the SEAD process is one of the most important decisions you'll ever make. It will allow you to free up your time, get out of the weeds, and let you focus on the high-impact work, thus increasing your chances of long-term success.

SEAD Benefit #2: Make More Money in Less Time

This may sound like hype, but it's absolutely true: SEAD can help you earn more while doing less. When you step out of the low-value, day-to-day tasks of your business, you free yourself to focus on work that actually moves the business forward.

Low-value tasks are anything that you can automate or delegate cheaply. As the business owner, your best use isn't packing boxes, fixing toilets, or entering data. It's in leadership, vision, or other high-output tasks that give you the best return on your time.

Once you get the low-value tasks off your plate and reclaim your time, you also create space for deep thinking and strategy. With less noise and stress, your mind is primed for insights and ideas to improve the business. The result is a flywheel. Less busywork leads to more clarity, and more clarity leads to better ideas. And those better ideas lead to a better, more profitable business that can further invest into automation, delegation, and systems, freeing up even more of your time.

SEAD Benefit #3: Love Your Business Again

Nobody likes *having* to do things. We enjoy *getting* to do things. But if your business depends entirely on you, then you *have* to get up and go to work every day, whether you want to or not. That obligation doesn't feel good, and you'll eventually grow to resent your business. Add into the mix being stuck doing tasks you dislike, and it drains you even faster.

SEAD helps remove the burden of you having to constantly be there and doing the tasks you hate. The result? You start enjoying business again, and it spills into every part of your life. You're a happier spouse, friend, and parent. And do you think you're more likely to have a successful business when you're excited to be there and enjoy what you do? Yup, me too.

SEAD Benefit #4: Amplify Your Impact

If you take pride in delivering a valuable product or service to your customers and want to help as many people as possible, you can't do it as a solopreneur or by building a business that orbits around you. No matter how talented you are, there are only 24 hours in a day. Without systems or a team, you become the bottleneck, limiting not only your revenue, but also the number of lives you can impact. Every person you could have served (but didn't) is now forced to either do business with an inferior competitor who doesn't care about them as much as you do, or to continue struggling with their problem.

To drive this home, imagine you discovered a cure for cancer. But you're the only one making the pills, and so at full capacity you can only churn out 100 doses per day. While saving 100 lives per day is meaningful, millions are left untreated. The tragedy isn't your effort—it's that your impact was capped far lower than it should have been because of how your business was built.

SEAD Benefit #5: Create a Stable Income

A business that depends on you is unstable. It's a castle made of sand, and either erosion or a wave will take it out. And an unstable business can't provide stable income.

Here's a reality few want to face: over time, your ability to work will decrease. It's inevitable. Whether it's a mental or physical decline, it eventually happens to all of us. That's why now is the best time to build a backup plan that allows you to generate revenue, even if you can't work.

Let's also not forget that unforeseen life events can strike at any time, giving us yet another reason to build a safety net. In 2016, my friend Russ developed a brain tumor that left him unable to think or work. Because his business depended on him, everything came crashing down, and to this day his abilities haven't fully recovered. His biggest regret? In his own words: "The one thing I wish I did more than anything else was create a business that doesn't require me to run it."

This is why you must make yourself replaceable. This is why you have to remove yourself as the linchpin and put systems, processes, and people in place. In this way, think of SEAD as the most valuable insurance policy you'll ever have.

On the other side of the coin, realize that instability doesn't just come from setbacks. Rapid, unexpected success can be just as dangerous.

A sudden flood of sales feels great until your systems can't handle it. Every weakness, bottleneck, and inefficiency gets exposed and amplified, potentially causing the entire system to collapse.

SEAD prevents this. By creating resilient systems, plugging leaks, and reinforcing points of vulnerability, you'll deliver more consistent results and ensure your business thrives through both storms and surges.

SEAD Benefit #6: Create a Valuable Asset

There's another downside to owning a job instead of a business: if you ever want to sell, you can't. At least for anything close to what you'd get for a bona fide business.

Jobs are liabilities, businesses are assets. And the only way to build an asset is to have systems, processes, and roles that are plug-and-play. Think about franchises: when someone buys a franchise, they're not buying the owner's hustle, they're buying a proven, replicable model. That's why franchises have higher success rates than independent startups.

Build your business with the same perspective and create an asset. Even if selling isn't on your radar yet, SEADing pays off right away with smoother performance, and later with a higher valuation, if you ever change your mind. After all, wouldn't you rather sell for full market value than for pennies on the dollar like most mom-and-pop shops that simply fade away?

SEAD Benefit #7: Get Your Life Back

I've saved the best for last. The number one reason to SEAD your business is to get your life back. You've heard it already but it's worth repeating: your business should serve your life, not steamroll it.

You shouldn't be taking business calls on date night or sneaking emails during your kid's birthday party. When your business is built right, you can show up fully for the moments that matter most and finally enjoy life without the worry that everything will collapse without you.

WHAT'S THE COST OF NOT DOING THIS?

Still not sure? I get it. Letting go of control can be scary, especially if you're used to being the one who holds everything together. I also know it can feel really weird to not be needed, or even—*gasp*—replaceable. But if you want a real business instead of a job, this is the shift you have to make. Face the discomfort head-on. Embrace it. Aspire to have your employees not miss you when you're on vacation. Or even better, not notice you're gone.

I'll be upfront: SEADing your business is an investment. It takes time, energy, patience, and a bit of money. You'll have to adopt a new way of viewing and thinking about your business. You'll need to develop a new set of skills, hire people, adopt new tools, and build infrastructure. At first, you may feel overwhelmed and it may even feel like you're going backwards. But I want to encourage you, keep going. The real cost isn't the effort, it's what happens if you don't.

What happens if nothing changes? Fast-forward five or ten years:

- *Are you still grinding, holding everything together by sheer willpower?*
- *What regrets will you have and what will have you missed out on in life?*
- *Will you still even be in business?*

Those are tough questions, and they're supposed to be. There's a lot at stake. More than most people ever realize. That's why SEAD isn't a "should." It's a must.

And that brings us to the heart of it: SEADing your business isn't just about profits or efficiency—it's about freedom.

CHAPTER 4:
WHY FREEDOM ISN'T OPTIONAL

love freedom and autonomy. I enjoy *getting* to do things, but I despise *having* to do things. Maybe it's my inner 8-year-old, but I'm not alone. Research shows that one of the strongest predictors of happiness is how much control people have over their own decisions. Christopher Morley nailed it when he said, "There is only one success—to be able to spend your life in your own way."

Naturally, when most people think about freedom, they picture the fun stuff: vacations, toys, and not having to punch a clock. And yes, those are all great, but they're only part of the picture. I believe freedom shows its greatest value when life throws you a curveball.

Most of the time, they're little things: your 10-year-old forgets to bring her lunch to school and you can bring it to her. Or your son gets sick and you can stay home with him for a couple days without worrying about work. Freedom keeps little disruptions like these from becoming big problems.

But sometimes, the curveballs are catastrophic; a car wreck, a serious illness, or loss of someone close. These events stop life in its tracks.

Several years ago, my mom called me out of the blue. We talked often, but I was usually the one who called, so I knew something was off.

"Hi Mom! How are you? What's going on?" There was silence.

She stuttered, "Honey...I have cancer."

"What? How bad is it?"

"Stage four. I have a seven percent chance of surviving five years."

It felt like the air had been sucked out of my lungs.

She told me she loved me and that it was going to be OK. (There she was, trying to comfort *me*, when she was the one with cancer. Typical mom, right?)

She promptly began treatment, and because of my flexible schedule, I was able to be there. I got to sit beside her as she received chemo treatment. We laughed. We cried. I was there to support her and I wasn't distracted by calls or worried about work. I was *present*. The freedom I'd set up in my business and the priorities I'd established allowed me to drop everything and be there for her.[2]

Now I don't know if you've ever had a situation like that with a loved one (hopefully not), but I can tell you, it changes you forever. You experience a sense of disbelief, denial, anger, sorrow, and loss; all at once. You feel the gut-wrenching ache of watching someone you love suffer, and realize your time together might be shorter than you expected. The fragility and fleeting nature of life are exposed in a raw, unapologetic way, and in that moment, you understand why freedom isn't optional. It's everything.

FREEDOM ISN'T JUST TIME AND MONEY

So what does freedom really look like? For most people, two things come to mind right away—money and time. And that makes sense. They're the most basic and visible kinds of freedom. Let's define them.

---

2   At the time of this writing, she's still in remission. Praise the Lord.

FINANCIAL FREEDOM

Financial freedom means having enough money to live the life you want without stressing over bills, gas prices, or a nice dinner out. At a basic level, it's simply having enough margin to live comfortably. At a higher level, it means having savings, retirement, investments, and maybe even living debt-free.

TIME FREEDOM

Time freedom means being in control of your calendar. It's the ability to sleep without an alarm clock, take a random weekday off because you feel like it, or go on an extended vacation without worrying. It's the difference between owning your time and your time owning you. Being on your calendar vs. someone else's.

Both financial and time freedom are crucial. Millions in the bank mean nothing if you're chained to your desk fourteen hours a day. And on the other side, endless free time isn't going to be as fun as you'd hoped if you're broke. You need both.

But the mistake most business owners make is they stop there. Money and time are *external freedoms* that can be tracked by your calendar and checkbook, but true freedom also requires *internal freedoms*, which are often overlooked but dramatically shape your experience of life and success. While external freedom gives you options, it's internal freedom that lets you enjoy them. You can have money in the bank *and* time on your calendar, but without emotional, mental, and health freedom, it won't be the experience you were hoping for.

EMOTIONAL FREEDOM

Emotional freedom is the ability to enjoy success without guilt, shame, or fear. If you feel guilty about doing well, or that you don't deserve it, or that it won't last, you'll never really enjoy it. If you judge yourself for wanting or having nice things, or for resting instead of hustling, you rob yourself of the joy your work was meant to provide.

Have you ever known someone who sabotaged their own success right as things were going well? Maybe they suddenly stopped showing up, burned bridges, or made irrational choices. Often the underlying cause wasn't a lack of competence, it was a lack of emotional freedom. Deep down, they didn't feel they deserved their success, so they destroyed it.

Emotional freedom allows you to pursue your vision unapologetically, to fully enjoy the rewards of your hard work, and live life on your own terms without constantly second-guessing yourself. It's the difference between just *having* success and actually *feeling* successful.

MENTAL FREEDOM

Mental freedom is the ability to prioritize what matters most, control your thoughts, and be fully present wherever you are. It's letting a high-paying client's call go to voicemail during a ball game with your family, without thinking twice. It's enjoying a board game with your kids and being fully there, without your mind drifting back to your to-do list.

Without mental freedom, you're always split. Your mind is in one place while your body is in another. You're halfway at work and halfway at home, which means you miss out on both. You're not effective at work, and you're not fully present at home. It's a no-man's land that leaves you constantly restless and unfulfilled.

HEALTH FREEDOM

Finally, there's health freedom: the ability to do what you want physically. For one person, it might mean walking on the beach without pain. For another, it could be playing on the floor with their grandkids. And yet for someone else, it might be running marathons or lifting heavy weights at the gym.

Health freedom looks different for everyone, but one truth remains the same: without it, everything else means less. What good is money if you're too sick to enjoy it? What good is time if you're in chronic pain? Confucius is credited with saying, "A healthy man wants a thousand things, a sick man only wants one."

Your health is the foundation for every other freedom. Lose it, and financial, time, emotional, and mental freedom all lose their value. That's why it's critical to approach your health with intention. Protect it. Invest in it. Because the freedom to live fully hinges on your ability to get up each day with the strength and energy to enjoy it.

KEY TAKEAWAYS

1. SEAD Helps You Take Your Life Back

The main goal of SEAD is simple: to create a business that supports your life instead of destroying it. When you design your business around freedom and flexibility, you can be present for the things and people that matter most, without sacrificing your livelihood.

2. SEAD Boosts Your Odds of Success

Most businesses fail due to time mismanagement, a lack of focus, or being overwhelmed by day-to-day demands. SEAD frees you to zero in on high-level priorities by putting systems and people in place, increasing your chances of long-term success.

3. SEAD Turns Your Job into a Real Business

If your business can't run without you, it's a job, not a business. SEAD helps you build systems and structure that make your company a true asset that you can sell, pass on, or step away from. It also acts as a contingency plan for life's curveballs.

4. A SEADed Business Gives You the Ultimate Gift: Freedom

Freedom is the real return on investment of a well-structured business. It doesn't happen by accident; it's something you intentionally design. Through elimination, delegation, and automation, SEAD gives you the freedom to spend your time and live your life as you choose.

5. The Cost of Not SEADing Is Steep

The price of doing nothing is high. Staying trapped in an owner-dependent business leads to stress, strained relationships, lost time, and eventually burnout or failure. Luckily, all of that is avoidable when you SEAD your business.

PART III

SEAD: S FOR STRATEGIZE

"Hope is not a strategy."

—Vince Lombardi

I was on a call with my friend Joe Turney, a successful real estate investor in Birmingham, Alabama. He was talking to me from the deck of his lakefront second home, where he often goes to relax. We were discussing his business, and I asked how he built his rental portfolio that fully funded his dream life.

"From the very start," Joe told me, "my plan was to create freedom. I didn't want another business that stole my time. I already had that, and I'll never go back."

This was Joe's third business. The first two (a software company and a marketing company) made good money, but they were filled with lots of stress, income swings, and long hours. He carried the scars to prove it: divorce, strained relationships, and a clear understanding of what *not* to do again.

So this time, Joe designed a business to fit around his life. He was no longer interested in just making a buck, and he didn't want a business that owned his schedule. He was so serious about this, he even told me, "If it came down to it, I'd take less income if it meant more freedom."

He continued, "Most people just start a business to make money, with no thought about how it will affect their life. I've made that mistake and won't do it again."

Joe's perspective is rare, but his mistakes aren't. Most entrepreneurs build a business that demands too many hours, strains their personal life, and depends on them for everything.

But as Joe proves, you don't have to follow that path. You can be intentional about how you create, structure, and run your business. And you're going to do it in reverse from what you might expect.

CHAPTER 5:
LIFE BEFORE BUSINESS

Before we dive into elimination, automation, and delegation, we need to start with strategy. We strategize first because it's the filter that determines how the E, A, and D steps look.

Because this is a business book, you might be expecting me to say that your strategy needs to include a detailed business plan, SWOT analysis, a stack of key metrics, precise forecasts, and budget estimates, right?

Well, sorry to disappoint, but none of those are going to be our starting point. *Gasp.* I know—business-book blasphemy. Instead, I want to propose something you may have never considered before. You may even want to sit down for this. Ready? Here it is:

Your strategy should be built on your life vision—not a business plan.

In other words, you're going to build and run your business based on what you want your life to look like, not the other way around.

YOUR STRATEGY SHOULD BE BUILT ON YOUR LIFE VISION—NOT A BUSINESS PLAN.

THE SEAD PROCESS

Figure 5.1: *Strategy comes from your life vision. From there you Eliminate, then Automate, then Delegate, until your vision matches your reality.*

I'll wait a moment as you pick your jaw up off the floor and let that sink in. And yes, I recognize this may seem strange, foolish, or even absurd to you. This isn't exactly what they teach in business school.

But there's a very simple reason to do it this way: If the point of owning a business is to give you the life you want, then you first need to know what that life looks like. (Cue the harp sounds of enlightenment.) After all, you can't design and run a company that serves your dream life if you create a nightmare business. Only after you have your vision in hand can you build a business that fits your life instead of fights with it.

Now to be clear, I'm not saying your business gets a hall pass from all the realities of running a profitable company. It still has to generate income, stay competitive, and deliver value to customers. What I *am* saying is that all else being equal, you can both make the money you want *and* design your business to align with your life. They're not mutually exclusive.

CREATING YOUR LIFE VISION

The next obvious question you may be thinking is, *OK, smart guy…what is this life vision thing? And how do I create one?* Great questions. The process I'm going to share with you is one I learned back when I was a client in a coaching organization called Lifeonaire.[3] The name of the company conveys the mission: to help people create rich and abundant lives.

Put simply, your life vision (vision for short) is the detailed blueprint for your dream life. It includes what you want to do and have, how you want to live, and who you want to become. It reflects your values, passions, priorities, sense of calling, and identity. In short, it's your north star for everything that makes up the life you desire.

To create your vision, paint the picture of what a perfect life looks like to you in every area. Here are a few suggestions to get you started:

- **Family:** What do your family relationships look like? What kind of spouse, parent, sibling, etc. are you?
- **Friends:** What kind of friends do you want? How do you show up for them? How do you interact with each other?
- **Health:** How do you feel physically, mentally, and emotionally?
- **Hobbies/Interests:** How do you spend your free time? What activities are you doing that bring you joy and fulfillment?
- **Giving:** What are you doing to be charitable? Where and how are you giving of your time, talents, or treasures?
- **Faith:** What does your spiritual life look like?

---

3   I believe in Lifeonaire so much that I now own the company.

Here's the rub though: creating a vision that's clear, authentic, and actionable takes work. It's not something you can just whip up in a few minutes, or even a few hours. It requires honest reflection and deeper thinking than most people ever do. Zig Ziglar once said, "Many people spend more time planning a two-week vacation than they do planning their life." Based on my experience, he's spot on.

After working with thousands of people from all backgrounds, I've met many who *thought* they had a clear vision, but after a little digging, realized they didn't. In more situations than I can recall, after I've asked someone what they want their life to look like, I'd get a response like: "I want to make $250,000 per year, drive a Mercedes, have no credit card debt, own a rental property, and travel a couple of times a year." And all those are great. Problem is, that's more of a balance sheet statement. It doesn't tell me how they want to *live*.

This doesn't come with any judgment, because most people were never taught the importance of having a vision. (Did you have a vision class in high school or college? Yeah, me neither.) The tragedy, however, is that not having one almost guarantees you'll have a life far short of what it could be.

RELEGATING YOUR VISION

Unfortunately, instead of investing focused time and effort to create their own vision, most people simply default to what others want for them. Sometimes that influence comes from family, sometimes from friends, and sometimes from society at large. Until I was 41 years old, almost every phone call with my mom included some version of: "Jason, you've spent so much time in school. You have a PhD. Why aren't you running a lab? How about being a professor? Have you looked into biotech?" She meant well and was only trying to help, but she was projecting her ideas of success onto me.

Maybe you've had a similar experience: people with good intentions offering friendly advice like "You should be an attorney…an engineer… an accountant…a *whatever*."

Or sometimes it's not advice at all—it's straight-up pressure. Maybe your parents are physicians, so you're expected to be one too. Or you're supposed to take over the family business when your parents retire. In those cases, others have decided your life for you.

I had a friend who loved working with his hands and wanted to be a carpenter. He came from a white-collar family, and his parents flat-out told him, "We are not carpenters in this family. We're better than that." *Ouch*.

And if family and friend influences aren't enough, society piles it on too. Many people choose careers based on status, significance, or financial rewards. Without a vision, it's easy for those things to suck you in like a Death Star tractor beam. You end up chasing approval, recognition, and money instead of your own deeper desires.

Please know I'm not throwing stones. I understand the appeal. I also know how hard it is to stray from the expected path. You might be looked at as crazy, gossiped about, or even shunned. People won't understand. When I had my government contracting job, I appeared successful to others. It looked like I *made it*. And when I stepped away, people thought I lost my mind.

And that's the bottom line: if you don't create your own vision, someone else will gladly hand you theirs.

THE JONESES ARE BROKE AND UNHAPPY

There's one more sneaky influence that can quietly hijack your vision: those infamous next-door neighbors—the Joneses.

If you're not careful, comparison slips in and takes over. Instead of running toward *your* goals, you'll get pulled into chasing *theirs*. If they have a bigger house, nicer cars, or take more lavish vacations, you think they're "winning" and you're "losing." Without a vision, you default to their standard of success instead of your own.

Sally and Bob got a new Acura? I'm going to get a Mercedes.

Jeff and Stacy went to Cancun? Fine. Maldives it is. First class.

Never mind they may be miserable behind closed doors, completely broke, and drowning in debt, you follow along anyway. On and on it goes, usually without a finish line, because you haven't defined success for yourself.

Now don't get me wrong. There's nothing wrong with nice cars, luxury trips, or beautiful homes. But "things" won't give you purpose or meaning. They also won't fix other broken parts of your life. You can only do those things by having and pursuing your vision.

There's also a hidden cost to "one-upping." Outwardly you look like you're winning, but inwardly you feel a void. You're stacking up trophies by society's scoreboard, but your soul is eroding. You'll be surrounded by a lot of stuff, but have no sense of peace, joy, or fulfillment. And the further down the road you get, the worse it gets.

I've talked to thousands of hard-working achievers who've spent years, even decades, chasing what they thought was the prize, only to discover they've been running a race they never wanted to win. And instead of joy and pride, they felt regret. Regret over lost time and missed chances to focus on what mattered most.

YOUR LIFE AND BUSINESS ARE CONNECTED

One final reason why a clear life vision matters is because your life and business are linked. You can try to separate them, but you can't. They exist together and influence each other in unavoidable ways.

- If your health is poor and your energy is low, will that affect your ability to work? *Of course.*
- If your relationships at home are strained, will that distract you from being your best at work? *Yep.*
- If you're overwhelmed in your business, will that stress follow you home? *Absolutely.*

You don't live in separate boxes. You carry your life into business and your business into your life, whether you want to or not. That's why defining your vision is so critical. It will allow you to show up at your best in both worlds.

CHAPTER 6: PUTTING YOUR VISION INTO ACTION

Have you ever stopped to really look at how most people spend their time? It's hard to unsee once you do. The pattern might be painfully familiar: wake up, get ready for work, work all day (often at a job you don't enjoy), come home exhausted, decompress, squeeze in a sliver of "free time," then go to bed. Repeat Monday through Friday.

Weekends aren't much better. Instead of rest and relaxation, they're spent catching up on everything you didn't get done during the workweek: grocery shopping, mowing the lawn, cleaning the house, laundry, and all the other deferred errands. See Figure 6.1.

Pause for a moment and really think about that. How much time is left for the things you *want* to do? Each year, the Bureau of Labor Statistics publishes the American Time Use Survey[4], which tracks how Americans spend their days. According to the data, employed adults with young children have about 3.0 hours of daily leisure. That's it.

Now stretch that pattern across a career. If you work from age of 22 to 67[5], that's 45 years of largely the same routine. Decades of your healthiest, most energetic, most precious years, spent mostly working, commuting, and recovering, just enough to do it all again the next day.

---

4   https://www.bls.gov/tus/.

5   The age for full Social Security benefits if born in 1960 or later.

THE WORK-FIRST WAY

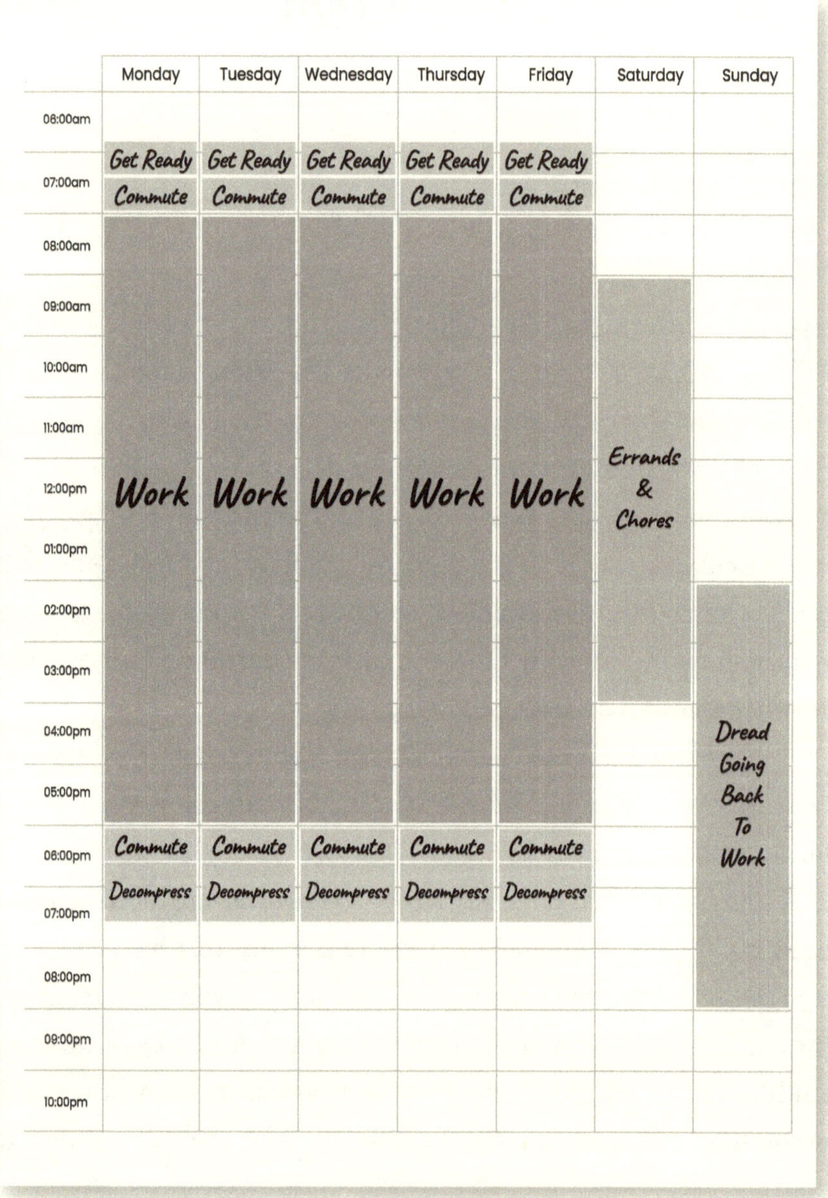

	Monday	Tuesday	Wednesday	Thursday	Friday	Saturday	Sunday
06:00am							
07:00am	Get Ready / Commute	Get Ready / Commute	Get Ready / Commute	Get Ready / Commute	Get Ready / Commute		
08:00am	Work	Work	Work	Work	Work		
09:00am	Work	Work	Work	Work	Work	Errands & Chores	
10:00am	Work	Work	Work	Work	Work	Errands & Chores	
11:00am	Work	Work	Work	Work	Work	Errands & Chores	
12:00pm	Work	Work	Work	Work	Work	Errands & Chores	
01:00pm	Work	Work	Work	Work	Work	Errands & Chores	
02:00pm	Work	Work	Work	Work	Work	Errands & Chores	Dread Going Back To Work
03:00pm	Work	Work	Work	Work	Work	Errands & Chores	Dread Going Back To Work
04:00pm	Work	Work	Work	Work	Work		Dread Going Back To Work
05:00pm	Work	Work	Work	Work	Work		Dread Going Back To Work
06:00pm	Commute	Commute	Commute	Commute	Commute		Dread Going Back To Work
07:00pm	Decompress	Decompress	Decompress	Decompress	Decompress		Dread Going Back To Work
08:00pm							
09:00pm							
10:00pm							

Figure 6.1: *When work is put on the calendar first, life gets the leftovers.*

And the most unsettling part is that most don't even blink at this schedule. It's unconsciously accepted as normal and followed by default rather than by design.

LIFE BY DESIGN

We already know the previous approach doesn't work if you want to have a life that is all it could be, so let's flip it. Instead of fitting life into the leftover cracks around work, put your vision items on your calendar *first, then* make work fit into what time remains.

I was first introduced to this idea at a Lifeonaire Get-a-Life Getaway event when I was still a client. After we finished the first draft of our visions, the instructor handed us a blank weekly calendar and said:

"Take what you wrote in your vision, and put it onto your calendar. Don't filter it or worry about your current schedule. Just write down what you'd *want* to do and when."

I stared at my paper, unsure where to begin. The instructor sensed my hesitation. He glanced at my vision and saw "working out at the gym."

"How often?" he asked.

"Four times a week."

"For how long?"

"About an hour-and-a-half."

"And what's your favorite time to go?"

"Three p.m., after I'm done working for the day."

"Would you still go at that time if you didn't have to work?"

"Um, yeah. All my friends are there, and I like working out with them."

"Great. Put it on the calendar."

So on Monday, Tuesday, Thursday, and Friday, I wrote down a 90-minute block that said "Gym."

Ahh, I think I get it, I thought.

I then added date night with my wife once per week.

Lunch with a friend once per week.

Thirty minutes of quiet time each morning.

One by one, I wrote down everything from my vision and when I wanted to do it. Even afternoon naps (*you better believe those went in*). Slowly, my calendar filled up until I couldn't think of anything else I'd want in my dream week.

When I finished, the instructor said: "Now add up all the empty spaces. That's how much time you have left for work."

I counted: about 25 hours.

And that's when it hit me like a ton of bricks.

For the first time, I realized I was living my life backwards. Without even thinking about it, I had been putting *work* first and *life* second. No wonder my personal time kept getting squeezed out. I had never considered this reverse approach before. This was the moment I understood clearly: **Your life vision—not your business demands—should determine how much time you have available for work.** See Figure 6.2.

THE LIFE-FIRST WAY

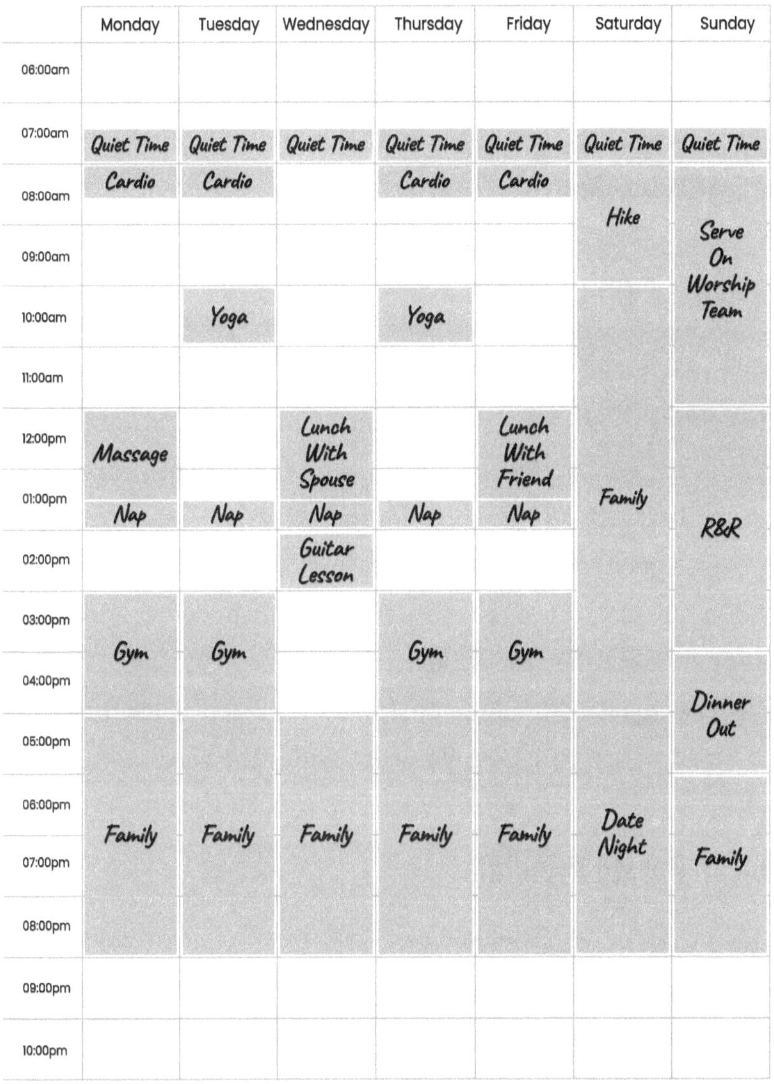

	Monday	Tuesday	Wednesday	Thursday	Friday	Saturday	Sunday
06:00am							
07:00am	Quiet Time	Quiet Time	Quiet Time	Quiet Time	Quiet Time	Quiet Time	Quiet Time
08:00am	Cardio	Cardio		Cardio	Cardio	Hike	Serve On Worship Team
09:00am							
10:00am		Yoga		Yoga			
11:00am							
12:00pm	Massage		Lunch With Spouse		Lunch With Friend		R&R
01:00pm	Nap	Nap	Nap	Nap	Nap	Family	
02:00pm			Guitar Lesson				
03:00pm	Gym	Gym		Gym	Gym		
04:00pm							Dinner Out
05:00pm							
06:00pm	Family	Family	Family	Family	Family	Date Night	Family
07:00pm							
08:00pm							
09:00pm							
10:00pm							

Figure 6.2: *Put the life you want on your calendar first, then design a business to support it.*

I realize this may sound like I'm saying the earth is flat, because we've been trained to believe that business demands should dictate our hours. But here's the problem with that: there's *always* something to do. You know this to be true. "Catching up" is a lie. It's a myth. There will *always* be one more email, one more call, one more opportunity. And if you try to keep working until every good idea is executed and every to-do item is completed, you'll be working a few lifetimes straight, without any lunch or bathroom breaks.

CAN I REALLY WORK LESS?

Once you see how a vision works, the next question, dripping with justified skepticism, is: *"C'mon…are you kidding me? I'm working 60-plus hours now and not making the money I want. How in the world can I make enough if I only work a fraction of that?"*

And I get it. The first time I drafted my vision, I felt the same way.

Do me a favor though: suspend your disbelief for just a moment. I'm going to make the case—like a trial attorney arguing to a jury of one (you)—that this is completely possible. I'll present a few pieces of "evidence" to convince you, then you can render the verdict. Fair?

Exhibit A: Pareto Principle

Let's start with the Pareto principle, also known as the 80/20 rule. This principle applies in almost every area of life and business. It began in 1906 when Italian economist Vilfredo Pareto noticed that 20 percent of landowners owned 80 percent of the land. Since then, it's been observed and proven again and again: a small percentage of causes creates an overwhelming percentage of results.

In business, it often looks like this:

- 20% of your customers generate 80% of your revenue
- 20% of your marketing attracts 80% of your clients
- 20% of your customers make 80% of the service requests

Of course, not everything follows that ratio exactly, but the general premise holds true; most outcomes come from a few key factors.

Now, let's apply this to your workweek. For a 40-hour workweek, the principle suggests that just eight hours (20 percent) are responsible for 80 percent of your results. Read that again and let it sink in: *Just eight hours a week are responsible for 80 percent of your results.* That means less than two hours of your day are producing over three-quarters of your business revenue and progress. Crazy, right?

This also means two other things: first, the majority of your time (the other 32 hours) is spent on tasks that don't really move you forward. And second, you don't need to grind out 40, 50, or 60+ hour weeks to run a successful business.

What you *do* need is the ability to identify and double down on the few "20 percent tasks" that move the needle the most in your business—a concept we'll address later. For now, just sit with this reality: more hours don't equal more impact. The right hours equal more impact.

Exhibit B: Parkinson's Law

In 1955, Cyril Northcote Parkinson published an observation around work management.[6] It states: "Work expands so as to fill the time available for its completion." Real talk? If you have 60 hours per week available for work, you'll stretch the tasks to fill 60 hours. Have 40, you'll get it

---

6   Cyril Northcote Parkinson, "Parkinson's Law," The Economist, November 19, 1955.

done in 40. And if you only have 20? You guessed it—you'll find a way to fit it into 20.

If you've ever worked a 9–5 job, you've likely experienced Parkinson's law without even realizing it. In most companies, you're expected to stay the full day no matter how much you get done. So, what do you do? You pace yourself, whether you realize it or not. Even though you *could* finish your tasks by lunch, you work slower, take more coffee breaks, check emails, and well, fill the time until the clock says it's time to go. If your boss said you could leave when your work is done, we both know you'd be out the door long before closing time.

Notice, Parkinson's law doesn't state that fewer hours equal less output. It simply says that work expands to the time given, which means the opposite is also true: when time is limited, work compresses.

This is one of the reasons I strongly encourage people to build their vision before their business. Your vision sets the bookends of your workday and gives you a reason to stop working. If you only have 20 hours per week available for work, you'll find a way to prioritize and focus in a way that gets the important things done within those 20 hours.

Exhibit C: Proof in the Data

A revealing 2017 poll done in the UK pulled back the curtain on how much time people really spend working.[7] Researchers surveyed 1,989 office workers and found that the average person was only productive two hours and 53 minutes per day. (If you have employees, you probably just nodded and whispered, *"Called it."*). Think about that…less than three hours per day produced *all* of the meaningful output from these workers. Not eighty percent. Not fifty percent. One hundred percent

---

7 https://www.vouchercloud.com/better-living/office-worker-productivity

of the output. And if you're counting, that's happening in 15 hours per week *total*…not 40.

Exhibit D: The Vacation Rush

Here's one last piece of supporting evidence that you can absolutely work fewer hours. This is my closing argument, which will bring the case home for sure.

Imagine you're leaving on a long-awaited vacation. You're boarding a cruise ship on Saturday morning. What happens the Friday before? You knock out more productive work that day than you did from Monday through Thursday combined. True or true? (Remember, you're under oath.)

How is this possible? Two simple reasons:

1. **You have to get it done**. You have a reason: There's no way you're going to miss that sweet tropical vacation.
2. **You focus on what matters most**. Maybe you don't finish every tiny task, but you get *the important things* completed—the ones that actually matter.

Now imagine approaching *every week* with that same clarity and urgency. What if everything in your vision functioned like your "cruise ship" (a compelling reason to focus and finish). Your vision shows you what's at stake and what you'll sacrifice when you work longer than your vision allows. Is it going to be date night with your spouse? The gym? Your kid's swim meet? Because every time you say yes to work, you're saying no to something else you've identified as important.

THE JURY IS IN

What do you think? Is it fair to say that working less might be possible? If the answer is yes, congratulations. You've just opened a new door of possibility. That single shift if belief is a massive step in the right direction.

And if you're still unsure, that's perfectly fine too. All I ask is that you *consider the possibility.* After all, remember that UK poll? Those workers logged less than three hours of real productivity per day, yet still accomplished the full output of their full 40-hour workweek. Not some. Not most. All of it.

Now I'm not suggesting you can (or should) slash your workweek from 60 hours to 20 overnight. That would be a great way to torch your business, and I've watched people do it. But over the span of a few quarters or a year, you absolutely can make huge progress.

The key to making this happen is changing how you run your business. And that's exactly where we're headed next.

CHAPTER 7:
WORK LESS, ACCOMPLISH MORE

I was a skinny kid growing up. I graduated high school at a whopping 142 pounds—soaking wet, shoes on, and with a roll of quarters in my pocket. I wasn't quite the Charles Atlas "sand-kicked-in-his-face" guy, but I wasn't far off either.

I hated being thin, so once college sports ended, I turned to lifting weights, hoping to build some muscle. I made some early progress, but as anyone who's ever worked out can tell you, a plateau is lurking around the corner. When mine hit, my "brilliant" solution to break through was to do more. More days. More sets. More exercises. I mean, if 15 sets weren't working, surely 30 would!

And for a very short time, it seemed like the answer—until everything came to a screeching halt. Not only that, I started backsliding. I was getting weaker, losing muscle, and looking worse. I felt tired and sore all the time, and even began hating the gym.

That's when I met Dante Trudel, creator of a training method called DC Training. His philosophy was the polar opposite of what I was doing. He advocated for short, intense, extremely low-volume workouts. I was skeptical because I couldn't wrap my head around how less could accomplish more.

I hired him anyway, and figured worst case, if it didn't work, I'd just lose a little bit of time, be out some cash, and could go back to my old way of training (even though it wasn't really working anyway).

A few days later, Dante sent over my new training program, and I quickly noticed what had to be a typo. On the program, he had me doing just one "rest-pause" set per body part. Not 15 sets, not 30. One. *You've got to be kidding me* I thought to myself. *How in the world am I supposed to get better results from just one set?!* That change in volume represented more than a 95% decrease compared with what I was previously doing. I expressed some concerns and he reassured me that while it would be an adjustment, I needed to trust the process.

He added in: "For this to work, you need to attack the weights like you're going to war."

"Yeah man. I get it. I already train hard."

"If you say so," he replied, with the exact tone you're imagining.

Skeptical but optimistic, off to the gym I went, new workout in hand. I got psyched-up and did my one rest-pause set, pushing as hard as I could. The moment I finished, my thought was, *That's it? Are you serious?* I felt like I'd just finished my warm-up and still had a full tank of gas. But Dante had made me promise I wouldn't add extra sets, so I left frustrated. I called him.

"Hey man, I think something's wrong. I wasn't tired at all."

"Sounds right," he replied. "You're used to pacing yourself over a boatload of sets. You don't know how to give focused, intense effort yet. Keep trying."

Although a bit offended, I humbled my ego and decided to listen. For weeks I left the gym frustrated, grumbling and convinced I was wasting my time. Then one day, something clicked. I pushed myself so hard in that single set that I couldn't have done another if my life depended on it. The switch had flipped.

What do you know?! Dante was right, I thought to myself.

I'd been so accustomed to spreading my energy out over my marathon workouts that I didn't know how to sprint. I finally learned to take all that paced effort and channel it into one single set. And the results? Game-changing.

Over two years, I gained close to 40 pounds of muscle, won state and national bodybuilding titles, and was featured in major fitness magazines. MTV even invited me to coach a young bodybuilder on their show *Made*. (I had to turn it down because I still had my full-time job. I guess America wasn't ready for me to be the next Jillian Michaels.)

LOW-VOLUME, HIGH-OUTPUT BUSINESS

Right about now, you may be thinking, *Okay Wojo…nice gym story. But what does any of this have to do with business?*

Answer: everything.

Most business owners fall into the same trap I did in the gym. They think that more is better. More hours, more hustle, more busyness. But just like adding set after set, piling on hours usually leads to the same outcome: wasted effort, diluted focus, and squandered time, all of which eventually point to burnout and stagnation.

Most entrepreneurs work like high-volume lifters: doing way too much, feeling proud of "grinding," yet confused why they've plateaued or even slid backwards. The truth? You could be working less and getting better results.

There is a catch. One of the keys to Dante's program that I didn't mention was that it focused on big, powerful, important movements—the hard ones that produce real growth. Heavy squats. Deadlifts. You get it. Not the fluffy pink dumbbell stuff. The same is true in business. You don't need to check off a 27-item to-do list. You need to attack the few activities that actually move the needle and "build muscle" (i.e. generate profits).

If you want to work fewer hours *and* still earn the money you want, this shift is a must. You need to stop trying to make up for inefficiency and ineffectiveness with sheer hours. And believe it or not, sometimes long hours are a form of laziness. When you're always "busy," it usually means you haven't taken the time to build systems or processes to free up your time. You haven't thought hard enough or long enough about better ways to run your business.

CHAPTER 8:
YOUR HIGHEST AND BEST USE

When starting a new business, it's normal to do almost everything yourself: sales, marketing, fulfillment, customer service, billing, bookkeeping…you name it. You're like a Swiss Army knife one-size-fits all solution, hacking away at tasks you don't like, aren't that good at, and aren't the best use of your time. This happens because you don't have the money to hire help yet.

You're also probably working a lot more hours than you'd prefer. Fueled by adrenaline, caffeine, and fear, you're doing whatever it takes to get things off the ground. And all this is fine, at least in the short term.

The danger comes when you stay in that mode too long. If you keep doing too many tasks and working too many hours, both you and the business eventually will start to suffer. You become the bottleneck due to your own personal capacity and skill limitations, and the business hits a ceiling. Ironically, the same hustle-and-grind DIY approach that helped you launch the business will later be the thing that causes it to stall. At some point, you must make the shift from doing all the work to doing the right work.

CHOOSING YOUR TASKS

Surprisingly enough, figuring out what you should be doing in your business isn't quite as simple or straightforward as you might think. The reason is because everyone's vision is different. This means there is no one-size-fits-all prescription, and no right or wrong. Still, there are three frequently used filters to help you decide:

1. What you enjoy
2. What you're good at
3. Highest-and-best-use (HBU) activities

WHAT YOU ENJOY

Even if you only work part-time hours, I believe you should enjoy as much of what you do as possible. Not everyone agrees, however. Some only care about how much money they make. And that's totally fine. But in my experience, enjoyment and performance are closely linked.

When you enjoy something, you naturally give more effort. For example, I love playing guitar. I'll pick it up to play for "just a few minutes," and next thing I know, two hours have passed. And because of that, I've logged thousands of hours and become pretty good.

The same dynamic applies to business. If you enjoy your role, you'll invest more energy, and over time you'll likely outperform others who are simply grinding through tasks they dislike.

Back in my PhD days, I did what was required to graduate, but I didn't *love* working in the laboratory. I wasn't dreaming up experiments in my free time or fantasizing about being published in esteemed journals. I just didn't have that deep passion.

Meanwhile, some of my classmates lived for the lab. They just couldn't get enough. They ate, breathed, and slept research. If I had chosen a career in science, they would have left me in the dust. That's why it's very hard to compete with someone who loves what they're doing. The job never feels like work to them, and they'll go the extra mile without even thinking about it.

To figure out what you enjoy, simply ask yourself: *On a perfect workday, what would I be doing? Would I be neck-deep in spreadsheets? Meeting clients? Creating content? Building strategy?* Whatever it is, that's a clue of where you should consider focusing.

I say *consider* because there's an elephant-sized catch here: If you choose tasks that don't add real value to the company, you're putting yourself at a significant disadvantage. You'll cap growth and struggle to stay competitive. Let's say you own a bakery and love baking cookies. That's fine, but as the owner, if you spend all your time over the oven, who's steering the business?

Now, you might think, *"I'll just hire someone to handle the other business stuff."* And in theory, this sounds great. But in practice, you may not have the cash because you're doing the minimum-wage work.

Please know I'm not trying to poo-poo on loving what you do. Far from it. I'm saying you need to temper it with reality. Joy matters, but it must be paired with impact.

Here's my best advice: the most rewarding and sustainable way to enjoy your business isn't by chasing the fun or easy tasks. It's by learning to embrace the challenge of the hard, valuable, strategic ones. Learn to love learning and getting better. Learn to love building your skillset so you can create a bigger impact and better results. Find joy in developing your team and serving your customers with excellence. And above all, savor the freedom, fulfillment, and opportunities that only a well-run business can give you.

WHAT YOU'RE GOOD AT

Your natural strengths and existing skillset are another filter for choosing your work, but the same warning applies: being good at something doesn't automatically make it valuable. It can even be a liability if it distracts you from what's important.

On the other hand, I also need to say, don't dodge important tasks just because you're not good at them yet. As the owner, you'll sometimes have to step into areas you're uncomfortable or inexperienced with because they're choking growth, and ultimately, you're the one responsible for fixing them. You don't have to become an expert overnight. Just start where you are and work at it until it's no longer a weakness.

As a bonus, later, when you later delegate these roles, your experience will help. You'll know what good looks like, be able to set realistic expectations, and train your team with credibility because you've done it yourself.

So yes, lean on your strengths whenever possible, but make sure they are relevant to moving the business along, and don't shy away from the gaps. Oftentimes, the very skills you resist are the same ones that unlock the next level of growth in your business.

HIGHEST-AND-BEST-USE (HBU) ACTIVITIES

Every business has tasks that make a bigger impact than others. Remember my low-volume workout routine? It was the heavy, hard movements that produced massive results—not the foo-foo exercises. It's the same in business. Some tasks move the business forward an inch; others move you forward a mile. These mile-movers are your "highest-and-best-use" (HBU) activities. The ones that produce the most tangible results and move the ball furthest down the field.

The fewer hours you want to work, the more critical it becomes to focus on your highest-and-best-use activities. If you have 80 hours per week available for work (hopefully you don't, because of all the cool things on your vision), then yeah, you can be a bit more loosey-goosey with your time. But if you only want to work 20 hours per week, then you must focus on HBUs.

A problem I see is that too many business owners burn their best hours doing low-value tasks. They're doing things like bookkeeping, sending invoices, or tinkering with their website. Tasks like these should be automated or delegated. You're the most valuable person in the business, which means you need to be focused on the most valuable work.

Many business owners struggle financially not because of external factors like the economy or competition, but because they're doing the wrong work. It's financial self-sabotage.

Let's run the math:

Say you work 40 hours per week, and you spend half of them doing tasks you could hire out for $20 per hour. Doing them yourself feels like you "saved" $400.

Smart move, right?

But what if those same 20 hours could have been spent on $100 per hour tasks? That's $2,000 of value, which means you didn't save $400… you lost $1,600.

Over a year, that's $80,000. In three years? Nearly a quarter-million dollars.

This alone is why a lot of business owners stay broke. They're bleeding potential profits by working on the wrong things. They're doing the "fluffy" stuff instead of moving heavy slag iron.

And the cost isn't just financial. Every hour wasted is also an hour stolen from your vision. It's an hour you're not with your family, in the gym, or building the life you said you wanted. The price tag isn't just in dollars; it's in missed life.

Philosopher Jim Rohn nailed it perfectly. When a man told him he'd bought a television for $400, Rohn replied, "No. The TV didn't cost you $400. It cost you about $40,000 per year because of what else you could do with that time." Low-value tasks carry the same hidden price and cost far more than you realize.

My mentor Steve Cook modeled this. In his first two years as a real estate investor, he closed 102 deals. When I asked how, his answer was simple: "While everyone else was worrying about their business name, their logo, and their spreadsheets, I was out there making offers." That's what focusing on HBUs looks like.

What is the equivalent of 'making offers' in your business? What are your highest value activities?

Taking HBUs even further, what is the *single* problem that, if solved, would unlock the next level of growth? What is the one constraint that has a chokehold on your business at this specific moment? This is your MVP (Most Valuable Priority), and if you want to move forward the fastest, *is the single area* where you need to focus. Maybe it's a weak lead pipeline. Maybe it's a poor sales conversion. Maybe it's broken fulfillment. Fix that first, *then* move to the next MVP. As you solve one problem, a new one appears behind it. It's a constant game of leapfrog. If you have a leads problem, then fix it, next you might see a sales issue. Then once you solve that, you notice that fulfillment needs attention. The MVP is always evolving, but at any moment, there is only *one* that matters most.

Right about now you might be thinking, "*I know what my problem is, but I don't have the time to fix it,*" or "*I don't have the skills to fix it.*" Don't worry. As you continue to SEAD your business, you'll free up time and resources to zero in and overcome these issues.

TRACKING YOUR TIME AND VALUE

In a previous life, I was a fitness and bodybuilding coach. People paid me good money to get them in the best shape of their lives. Sometimes it was for the competition stage, and other times just to feel and look better. I loved watching how their physical progress changed the way they saw themselves and the world around them.

Because measuring progress starts with knowing your starting point, the first assignment I gave every new client was to write down everything they ate for an entire week. Yes, *everything*. And 99 times out of 100, people were shocked when I ran the numbers. What they thought they ate was worlds apart from reality.

Apply this to work and be prepared to be blown away. Tracking your time will reveal your true work habits and explain in a large part the results you've gotten. It will also shine a light on what needs to change. Yes, tracking is a hassle, and yes, tracking is annoying. But it's also one of the most eye-opening and powerful things you'll ever do in your businss to shape your productivity.

Time tracking will show you:

- **Total hours worked.** Are you working within the hours your vision allows?

- **Task quality.** Are you spending time on high-payoff work or wasting it on busywork?
- **Focus.** How long are you able to focus on a single task before getting distracted and switching?
- **True hourly value.** What is the average hourly wage of the tasks you're doing?

On the last point, tracking your time will reveal whether your average hourly wage is enough to fund your vision. For example, if your vision requires $100,000 per year, and you want to work 25 hours a week for 40 weeks, your average wage needs to be at least $100/hr. (25 hours x 40 weeks = 1000 total hours of work, then divide that by $100,000). Make sense? (It actually has to be a bit higher after figuing in taxes.)

And again, I know you'd probably rather get a root canal than write down everything for a week, but the clarity you'll gain will make the aggravation worth its weight in gold. The following steps will help guide you through this simple process.

Step 1: Capture Everything You Do in the Business

For one full week, write down *everything* you do in your business. Record your activities either every time you switch tasks, or every 15 minutes (whichever is shorter). Don't wait until the end of the day because your numbers will be way off.

Use any method you want: a time-tracking app, a spreadsheet, or even a pen and paper. What matters is accuracy. For each activity, note:

- The specific task
- The start and end time

You may be tempted to leave off activities you know weren't work: surfed social media for 10 minutes, browsed motorcycle helmets on Amazon for 15 minutes, watched a few YouTube shorts. Don't leave these out. It's like my fitness clients who "forgot" to mention the 4 candy bars they woofed down, meanwhile I'm wondering why the diet isn't working. Tracking everything is key because it gives you the truth about where your time really goes.

Step 2: Calculate Your Average Hourly Wage

Once your log is complete, add a dollar value to each task. Ask yourself: *What would I have to pay someone else to do this?* Tasks that weren't work get a value of $0. Your numbers don't have to be exact; just get ballpark. If you don't know what something costs, a quick online search will help.

Now do the math to calculate your average wage:

1. Multiply the hours you spent on each task by its hourly rate.
2. Add those totals together.
3. Divide that number by the total hours worked.

Example (8-hour workday):

       3 hours @ $20/hr. = $60

       2 hours @ $100/hr. = $200

       <u>3 hours @ $35/hr. = $105</u>

       Total = $365

Then divide $365 by 8 hours = $45.63/hr. average wage.

With this information, you'll see exactly where your time is going and know what needs to change. You may also notice patterns:

- When you're most productive, and when you tend to drift. Maybe you're great before lunch but fade in the afternoon.
- When during the day you're better at different types of tasks (creative, analytical, or administrative). This is a chance to reorganize your task hitlist.
- What tasks should be eliminated, automated, or delegated.

CHAPTER 9: YOUR SEAD BLUEPRINT

Once you've created your vision, you now are ready to eliminate, automate, and delegate, in that specific order.

First, Eliminate. Ruthlessly cut everything that doesn't serve you or your business. If it doesn't move you toward your vision, it goes.

Next, Automate. Anything you do repeatedly that doesn't need a human gets handed off to systems or software. With AI, this list is growing by the day.

Lastly, Delegate. And finally, if a task requires a human touch, hand it off to a skilled person who can take it on.

To execute the steps smoothly, simply follow the questions Figure 9.1 below.

THE SEAD DECISION TREE

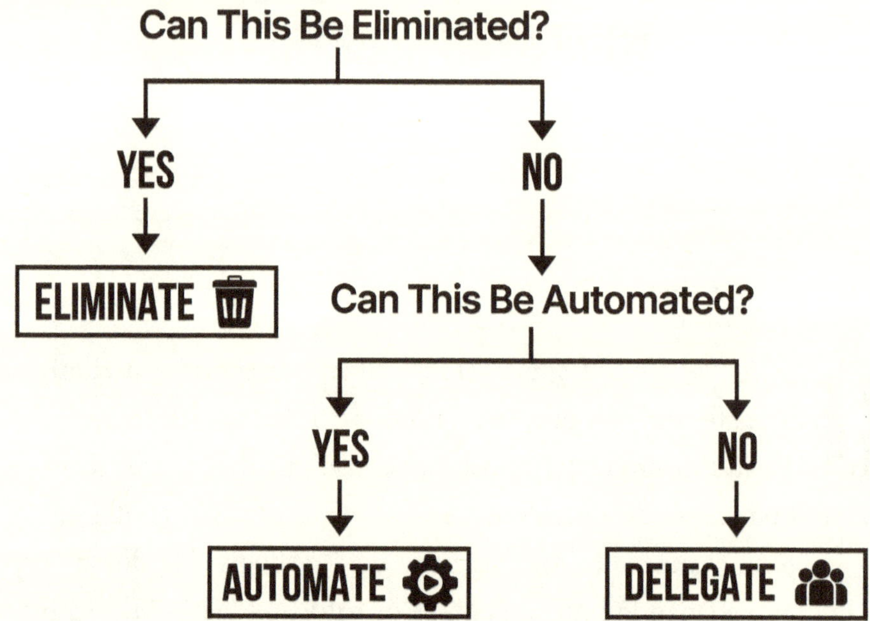

Figure 9.1: Elimination, automation, and delegation in that order saves resources and maximizes leverage.

CREATE YOUR BUSINESS ARCHITECTURE MAP

Before you can build the business you want, you must understand the business you have. That's where a Business Architecture Map (BAM) comes in.

Your BAM is an exploded-view diagram of your business that allows you to see how all the parts fit together. If you've ever put together a piece of furniture from IKEA, you've seen one of these: every nut, bolt, screw, and piece is drawn out to show how everything fits together. In the same way, your BAM shows how each role, responsibility, and task fits into your company.

The reason this is important to create is that once you have a complete picture of your business, it becomes much easier to decide what to eliminate, automate, or delegate. Without this map, SEADing your business will feel like trying to solve a jigsaw puzzle with all the pieces upside down.

HOW TO CREATE YOUR BAM

My preferred way to create a BAM is to use mind map software. Think back to those old tree diagrams you made back in high school. Same idea. They allow you to create branches between different items so that you can see how everything is connected. Maybe your grandmother made one for your family tree. Not a visual person? No worries, you can create your BAM in a document with nested bullet points. Either works.

Here's the step-by-step process:

Step 1: Map Your Departments

We start at the top and work our way down. Think broad to narrow. Even if you don't see your business as having "departments," it does. Departments are simply buckets that group similar activities together. Here are the most common ones:

- Operations
- Marketing
- Sales
- Finance
- Human Resources (HR)
- Tech (IT)

Keep it simple, but make sure each part of your business fits somewhere.

Step 2: List the Responsibilities

Next, list out everything that happens inside each department. Don't worry about *who* does the work or *how* it happens yet. Just record all the tasks and responsibilities.

Here's a glimpse of what that might look like for a finance department (this list is not exhaustive):

- Customer billing

  o Invoicing
  o Managing accounts receivable and collections
  o Tracking successful and failed bank transactions

- Bookkeeping

  o Syncing bank and credit card accounts
  o Categorize income and expenses
  o Approving or merging transactions
  o Reconciling monthly statements

- Reviewing the P&L, balance sheet, and other reporting
- Paying company credit cards
- Managing accounts payable
- Cutting affiliate commission checks
- Running payroll

Make sense? Not too bad, right?

BUSINESS ARCHITECTURE MAP (BAM)

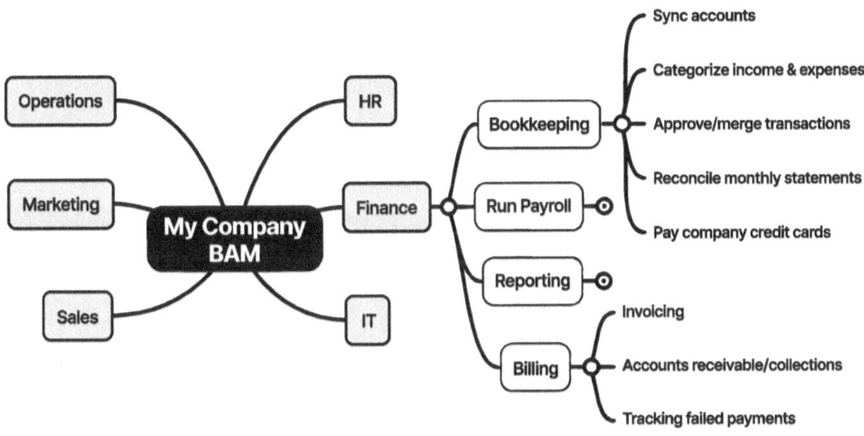

Figure 9.2: A BAM reveals opportunities for elimination, automation, and delegation. (Note: this BAM is incomplete. The small circles to the right are collapsed tree branches.)

Here's another example for a marketing department. I'll break down just "ads" here as an illustration, but you would do the same for the other marketing methods too.

- Ads

    o Write copy

    o Design graphics

    o Choose ad placements

    o Manage ad budget

    o Set up and run ads

    o Monitor campaign performance

    o Adjust ads based on metrics

    o Prepare reports for the team

Hopefully this is making sense and you're starting to get a feel for all the different parts of your business. Time spent creating your BAM is incredibly valuable, so it's worth the time. You don't need your list to be perfect on the first try. Just get it all out of your head and onto the page.

Step 3: Clarify How Things Get Done

You're doing great. Now identify how each task is currently getting done.

- Circle all the tasks *you're* personally doing
- Mark an "A" next to tasks that are currently automated
- Mark a "D" next to tasks that are already delegated (and to whom)

(Spoiler alert: your name will probably show up more than you'd like, but that's the point of this exercise. The goal is to expose reality so you can change it.)

Step 4: Label Each Task E, A, or D

Now comes the fun part: your first pass at SEADing your business. Now that you have a good grasp on all the tasks in your business and how they're currently being done, you can start moving toward what you want the business to look like in the future.

For *every single item* on your BAM:

1. First ask whether this should even exist. If the answer is no, write a large E beside the task, then circle the E to mark it for elimination.
2. Next, look at what remains, and label each item with a big circled A or D.

Again, this is just your first pass, so don't worry about it being perfect. As you work through the chapters on eliminate, automate, and delegate, keep your BAM nearby. With each chapter, you'll understand these steps better and can update your labels as your clarity grows.

TOP FIVE STRATEGY MISTAKES TO AVOID

Building the wrong business can be worse than building no business at all. Here are five of the most common mistakes in the Strategize step:

Strategy Mistake #1: Not Creating Your Own Vision

Remember: your business strategy is based on your life vision. This means you *must* invest the time to develop one. No one else can do this for you. If you allow others to define success for you, you'll never have the business and life you desire.

Strategy Mistake #2: Filtering Your Vision

Most people downsize their dreams before they even put them on paper. You may struggle to believe you can have everything you want. I get it. But I can also tell you that something magical happens when you write down what you really want and cast aside perceived limitations or restrictions. As a helpful trick, imagine you just won the lottery, and money is no longer a constraint. What would you do? How would you live day-to-day?

Strategy Mistake #3: Designing Your Business First

Many owners get swept up in the rush to start a business and tell themselves they'll create their vision later. But later never comes. Years later, they're pulling their hair out because they're buried in a business they hate. Do yourself a favor and create your vision first, *then* jump into the business. This will pay dividends in the success and sustainability of your business, as it will now serve your life instead of steal it. Already have a business? No worries, just create your vision ASAP before building your business further.

Strategy Mistake #4: Only Focusing on the Money

Profit matters, but it's not the only payoff of a successful business. Your business can also fulfill other parts of your vision. For example, if your spiritual life is important to you, find a way to include that in your business. Maybe you'll openly exhibit that faith in your branding. Or if charity is part of your vision, your business may support a local nonprofit. When your business reflects your vision, it becomes a source of meaning, not just money.

Strategy Mistake #5: Surrounding Yourself with the Wrong People

I haven't addressed this, but the people around you will either fuel your vision or fight it. Are they encouraging, supportive, and willing to challenge you to grow? Or are they critical, negative, and discouraging? The wrong people will slow you down and make it more difficult to achieve success. The right ones will accelerate your progress. Choose your inner circle wisely.

KEY TAKEAWAYS

1. Define Your Life Vision Before Your Business

Before designing your business, create your vision. This ensures the business aligns with and supports the life you want to live.

2. More Hours Aren't the Answer

More hours do not equal better results, and fewer hours don't mean worse results. If you're always busy, it's a sign something is broken in your business. Lean into Parkinson's law and the Pareto Principle to achieve better results in less time so you can enjoy a better work-life synergy.

3. Focus on High-Value Activities

Concentrate on the Most Valuable Priority (MVP) of the business and use data to identify and focus on the HBU tasks that impact business growth and profitability the most.

4. Create a Business Architecture Map (BAM)

Map out every role, responsibility, and task in your business. This provides clarity on current operations and opportunities for improvement. It also helps identify which activities should be eliminated, automated, or delegated.

5. Eliminate First, Then Automate, Then Delegate

Once you have your vision and BAM, you'll know how your business needs to be structured. From there, eliminate unnecessary tasks, automate repetitive processes, and delegate effectively—in that order. Collectively, these efforts will free up time and focus for high-value activities and personal priorities.

PART IV

SEAD: E FOR ELIMINATE

"Perfection is achieved not when there is nothing more to add, but when there is nothing left to take away."

— Antoine de Saint-Exupéry

Jimmy was your typical overworked business owner, juggling four different businesses and running himself into the ground. Most days he was up at 5:30 a.m. and working until 10 or 11 at night. The next day? Same thing. The day after that? Yup, you guessed it.

While he was doing well financially, he was experiencing the toll of the long hours on his personal life. The money didn't matter to him anymore, because he didn't have the time to enjoy it.

To get a grasp on things, we took a close look at all four of his businesses and discovered that one was eating up 50 percent of his time but only making 25 percent of his income.

He now had a couple of options.

Option A: If he simply eliminated that business, he could instantly free up half of his time and only lose 25% of his income. He'd get a huge chunk of life back.

Option B: Take a portion of the newly freed up time and invest it into his best business. Doing this would match, if not beat, his previous income with fewer hours.

Another great example of the power of elimination comes from John, an insurance agent in High Point, North Carolina. John is a sharp go-getter who is also blessed with some good ol' Southern charm. People like and trust him, and as a result, give him their business. Grateful for their patronage and wanting to honor their trust, John goes the extra two miles for his clients. He prides himself on his support, honesty, and knowledge.

This mixture of skill and heart led to rapid business growth. What started small quickly expanded into a massive client list that exceeded his capabilities to provide the red-carpet level of support he wanted—at least without creating serious consequences to his personal life.

He knew he had to do something, or things would go downhill quickly, both at work and at home. He decided to analyze his client list using three criteria: (1) who he enjoyed working with, that (2) provided a solid stream of income, and (3) had good growth potential.

What he found shocked him: 80 percent of his clients weren't bringing in enough money to justify the amount of time he was spending on them. Even worse, some were actually costing him money because they needed so much attention (if you have clients like this, you know the type). As a result, he was unable to focus on the top 20 percent of clients who were easier to work with, more enjoyable, and more profitable.

He had a tough choice: On one hand, he personally liked the 80 percent-ers (most of them, anyway). And even though they weren't his ideal clients, they still were a big chunk of his revenue. On the other hand, he couldn't shake the question of whether he could do better financially (and work less), if he were to only focus on his ideal clients.

He took a deep breath and made a bold move: he sold the entire 80 percent to another agent who was a better fit. Overnight, his client list shrank to just 20 percent.

What happened next was amazing. Yes, his revenue dropped dramatically at first. But the buyout money kept him steady while he rebuilt, this time only focusing on attracting his ideal clients.

The first thing he did was double down on making sure his remaining clients loved working with him. With the newly available time, he was able to pull out the white gloves and provide first-class service.

His clients noticed. They were happy with his level of service before, but now they were blown away. They started telling their friends, coworkers, and family. Referrals skyrocketed. And guess what? Most matched his ideal client profile because his "20 percent-ers" knew and associated with people just like themselves. Steadily and intentionally, he was able to rebuild his book of business. But this time it was with ideal clients who met his criteria, not the kind he didn't want but would've said yes to in the past, just to get the business.

As this process played out, his business, results, and income snowballed. Today, with fewer clients, John makes over twice what he used to and works only half days. His afternoons and evenings are his again. And every few years he prunes his client list again to raise the quality even higher.

I began this section with two very different stories of elimination to show just how wide and powerful it can be. Elimination isn't just about cutting tasks or canceling unused software. It can be applied to entire businesses, sections of a business, individual roles and positions, and even single steps in a process. Let's get into it.

CHAPTER 10:
WHY ELIMINATE?

Congratulations, you're ready to start eliminating. But before we dive in, here's a quick recap of how far you've come:

- You now see the importance of creating a business that can run without you being in every detail.
- You understand why you've been working so much
- You realize you can have both a thriving business and a great life, not just one or the other.
- You've written your vision and know both how much money you must earn to live it, and how many hours you have available for work.
- You've created your Business Architecture Map (BAM) and have a full overview of how your business operates.
- You've identified what you should be doing in your business and taken your first swipe at what can be eliminated, automated, or delegated.

Armed with this information, you're now ready for elimination. Remember, we do this first, because if you can get rid of something and it improves your business, there's no need to automate it or hand it off to someone else. That would be a waste of resources. We first "take away" by eliminating, then "give away" by automating and delegating.

Eliminating things from your business may not feel as exciting as automating or delegating, but it's every bit as powerful. Elimination improves performance, reduces complexity, and saves money—all at once. And unlike automation and delegation, which take money and resources, elimination is free and gives you them back.

Elimination is so important because unfocused and complex businesses often fail. They have too many plates spinning, try to do too much, and chase too many ideas. The result is that they never gain traction. David Packard, cofounder of Hewlett-Packard, put it perfectly: "More companies die from indigestion than starvation."

When this is the case, instead of making steady headway, results are scattered and inconsistent. Like a rocking chair, there might be lots of movement, but no forward progress. Elimination prevents this fate. The best way to get more done is to have less to do. By removing what doesn't belong, you narrow your focus, free up resources, and move faster. In contrast to a physical cut to your body that causes bleeding, this kind of cutting makes the bleeding stop.

In the field of medicine, there's a term called *minimum effective dose* that's useful in explaining how this plays out. MED is described as the least amount of a drug needed to produce a desired outcome. Anything less doesn't work. The same principle applies to business. If your time, energy, effort, and resources are spread too thin and you can't put in the minimum required input, you won't get the outcome you want. It's like trying to water twenty plants with only one small watering can. You can sprinkle a few drops on each and watch them all wither, or you can water a select few properly and watch them thrive. The only way to prevent this fate is to keep the best plants and get rid of the rest.

Let's dive into the benefits of elimination so you can see why you'll want to give it your full attention.

Elimination Benefit #1: Maximize Limited Resources

Every business, no matter the type or size, has limited resources. Time, money, energy, and attention are all finite. This means you must be ruthlessly selective when deciding where to allocate precious resources. Every product or service that's not generating outsized results is dragging you down.

Every time you say *yes* to one thing, you're automatically saying *no* to every other option. This is called *opportunity cost*, and you incur it with each choice you make. If you invest $10,000 into a postcard marketing campaign, that's $10,000 you can't use elsewhere in the business.

This principle applies just as much to time, energy, and attention. Every choice comes with a tradeoff, so you have to align all resources for their greatest return. Elimination is a powerful ally here. As you strip away low-value options and noise, it's easier to make better decisions and deploy limited resources for their greatest return.

Elimination Benefit #2: Do Less, But Better

As a business grows, so do disorganization and complexity. There's more to do, more responsibilities, and more moving parts. Small points of friction are amplified, weaknesses are exposed, and inefficiencies are multiplied. All of this translates into more chances for things to break, go wrong, or get neglected.

To make matters worse, this growth is also often accompanied by what I call *impulse adds,* which get tacked on because an opportunity presented itself.

It usually starts innocently. You run a painting business. But then one day, you get asked to install drywall because someone flaked. You figure, *Sure, it can't be that hard,* so you agree. You make some moola and so decide to offer both painting and drywall services. After a while you notice how much the flooring guys are making and so you start a flooring company. On and on it goes. Fear tricks us into believing we'll miss out on the next big thing or leave money on the table if we don't pursue that new opportunity. But the truth is, most times you're better off keeping your head down and pouring into what you already have.

It's like catching tennis balls. Throw one in the air and it's easy. But toss ten at once, and you're unlikely to catch any. The more things competing for your attention, the less likely you'll be able to succeed at any of them.

Eliminating is the antidote. By removing add-ons and everything but the best parts of the business, you realign the company with its core strengths. You and your team become more aligned, and confusion and distractions are minimized. As the quantity of moving parts decreases, quality increases. You do fewer things, but you do them better. It's addition by subtraction.

Elimination Benefit #3: A More Agile and Healthy Business

As you eliminate all but the best from your business, you'll often make more money. This happens because you're not only cutting costs in areas that aren't producing, but also doubling-down on the ones that are. This translates directly to the bottom line and results in a financially strong business.

And it can happen fast. A major benefit of elimination is speed. Getting rid of something can produce results almost instantly. Both automation and delegation take time and have more steps. Automation requires you to build, test, and launch. Delegation requires you to find, hire, onboard, and train team members.

A streamlined business can pivot rapidly based on changing market conditions, consumer trends, or unexpected challenges. In other words, when times get tough, a simple company is more likely to survive. And when demand spikes, a lean business can adjust quickly because simplicity scales easier than complexity.

CHAPTER 11: ENEMIES OF ELIMINATION

Hopefully you now see the power of elimination. But knowing the benefits isn't the same as doing it. Two enemies often keep entrepreneurs from fully embracing elimination: the entrepreneurial spirit itself, and fear.

Elimination Enemy #1: The Entrepreneurial Spirit

The first factor that makes eliminating a challenge is, ironically, the very same trait that can make a business owner successful: the entrepreneurial spirit.

Entrepreneurs are creative, driven, and good at spotting opportunities. They are used to chaos, won't take no for an answer, and can be overly optimistic. These qualities make entrepreneurs amazing, but they're also a double-edged sword. Those same strengths often lead to short attention spans, shiny object syndrome, and the temptation to chase too many ideas at once. The thrill of starting something new feels better than the slower, less exciting work of finishing or refining. Translation? The owner drifts from idea to idea, and none of the projects ever get the time they need to really thrive. I mean, heck, this tendency even shows up in the word itself: *entrepreNEWer*.

I see it all the time: "serial entrepreneurs" with nothing to show for their work other than a collection of half-baked businesses, none running near full potential. I know because I used to be one of them. Early in my journey, I was running several businesses at once. All of them relied on me, and none made the money I knew they could. My time and energy were too diluted, and nothing gained traction until I started to eliminate.

To be clear, I'm not against having multiple businesses. The problem is when they're built at the same time and they all rely on you. Splitting your resources across several ventures almost always leads to added stress and weaker results.

You've got to grasp this reality: the flow of ideas and opportunities will never stop. And just to prepare you, the more successful you become, the more frequent, relentless, and seductive they get. As your reputation grows, people will line up to pitch partnerships, deals, and investments. As your skills sharpen, you'll spot more gaps in the marketplace and think, *I could make money there.*

All these might even be things that just a short time ago, you would have cut off your left arm for. But now you have to say no. You must ruthlessly reject everything but the very best, highest return ideas, or risk a slow death by distractions.

So, how do you stay focused? Have a clear vision. It's the filter that tells you whether an opportunity moves you closer to goals, or whether it's just another distraction disguised as an opportunity. Unless it gets you to your vision faster or more easily, you have to give it a hard pass.

Elimination Enemy #2: Fear

Part of the reason I had multiple businesses early on was me craving variety. The other part? Plain ol' fear. My first business wasn't making the profits I thought it should, and for some reason, I thought starting more businesses was the way to make more money. I also justified this decision by telling myself it was smarter to diversify my income streams than have all my eggs in one business basket.

Here's how it worked out: Instead of having one underperforming business, I suddenly had three. And embarrassingly enough, this number ballooned even further before I realized this approach wasn't working.

Looking for help, I got some coaching and explained my situation.

His advice was simple: "Pick one and axe all the others."

"Which one?"

To which he replied, "They're all good businesses. Any of them will work if you just focus on it."

I hated his answer. My ego didn't like it either because it loved the image of being a hotshot entrepreneur with multiple companies. But I also had to face the reality that my strategy wasn't working.

I finally put my fear, ego, and skepticism aside, and decided to listen. I shut down one of the businesses. And wouldn't you know it, the ones that remained started doing a bit better. *Huh. Look at that.* Encouraged, but still unsure if it was just a fluke, I closed another. And again, performance improved. Finally convinced that my coach might be right, I got rid of all but one business, and that was the turning point where my income shot up and my stress levels went down.

Looking back, I thought my biggest fear was choosing the wrong business to keep. And yes, that fear was real. But what I didn't realize was two other forces were also influencing my reluctance: loss aversion and the sunk cost fallacy. If you're struggling with eliminating parts of your business, these are likely affecting you too. Both trick you into protecting what should be cut.

Loss aversion says that we feel the pain of losing something about twice as strongly as the joy of gaining it. That means eliminating feels far scarier than it really is. Your brain exaggerates the pain of letting something go, even when it's holding the business back.

Combine that with the sunk cost fallacy, our tendency to stick with something simply because we've already invested time, money, or energy into it, and it's clear why we hold onto things too long. This is the same force that keeps people in bad investments, bad relationships, and bad businesses.

This is where it's important to recognize that eliminating something isn't a loss or an admission being wrong, it's pruning. A good gardener doesn't just pull weeds and dying plants. They also trim the healthy plants to encourage new growth. In the same way, pruning your business clears the space needed for something better to grow.

CHAPTER 12:
IDENTIFYING THE MUD

The entire idea behind eliminating is simple: keep the best, cut the rest. You're panning for gold. Sifting through the dirt and grime to find the valuable nuggets.

To make this easy, I came up with the acronym **MUD**. It stands for **meaningless, unnecessary, or distracting**. MUD is anything and everything in your business that doesn't (1) produce massively outsized returns, and (2) move you closer to your vision. Just like real mud on your car windshield makes it difficult to see the road ahead, MUD in the business blocks your view and slows you down. The more you clear away, the faster you can move.

How can you tell the difference between "the best" and "the rest?" Data. Elimination shouldn't be driven by gut feelings alone. Whenever possible, use data to guide you. Without data, you're guessing and more likely to make a poor decision. Data helps you stay objective. Still, don't let a lack of data paralyze you. If your numbers aren't complete or perfect, you still need to eliminate. Just be extra careful.

When you're ready to eliminate, leave no stone unturned. Put everything under the microscope, including:

- Entire divisions or branches of the business
- Roles, responsibilities, or recurring tasks

- Products, services, or offers
- Customers or clients who drain time or energy
- Tools, software, or equipment
- Even partnerships or relationships

Literally everything is a potential target to be removed, canceled, or shut down. If you're struggling with where to start, here are a few places to look:

REVIEW FINANCIALS

Your numbers are a treasure map that will lead you to some pretty amazing discoveries. Open your books and look at your profit and loss statement (P&L) and balance sheet. Go line by line, searching for areas where revenue is weak, profit margins are thin, or expenses are bloated. Are some products barely selling? Are your expenses or overhead out of control? Is the cost of goods sold (COGS) too high in some areas? Cut the losers so you can double down on the winners.

But remember: not every elimination decision needs to tie directly to finances, so don't only look here. Time, energy, attention, and alignment with your vision matter just as much.

EXAMINE NON-CORE ACTIVITIES

Most businesses start with one clear thing they do well. But as we discussed, over time, "add-ons" creep in. Many times, these side projects are a distraction and drain resources. They complexify the business. Check the numbers (demand, margins, time required) to see if they make sense to keep. If not, cut them.

GET CUSTOMER FEEDBACK

If you ask, customers will tell you what they value. You might offer ten different services, but they only care about three. Or maybe you offer a bundle deal, but after speaking with customers, you discover people really only want one of the items included. Listen. When you simplify what you offer, you often save money and increase sales at the same time.

ASK YOUR TEAM

Your team lives in the details and sees things you don't. This means they have an excellent vantage point to share their experiences and make recommendations. Ask them what they think could be simplified or nixed. What do they think is clunky, unproductive, subpar, or not in alignment with the company vision? Their answers might surprise you. (Hopefully they don't say "you!")

RECONSIDER YOUR RESOURCES

Take a hard look at your equipment, inventory, and even your staff roles. Are they truly adding value and helping push the business ahead? Or just adding cost and drag? Fewer, higher performing assets often outperform a bloated setup.

ASSESS MARKETING RESULTS

Marketing is one of the biggest places that businesses waste money. Not because it's not important, but because it's not measured. Analyze your marketing efforts across all platforms, and identify the poorly performing campaigns. If ads aren't converting, costs are too high, or leads are poor quality, either fix it or pull the plug.

CHAPTER 13:
THE ELIMINATION PROCESS

Now that you know what's on the chopping block, it's time to walk through *how* to eliminate. We're going to keep this simple with a three-step process:

Step 1: Find and screen potential items to eliminate

Step 2: Eliminate

Step 3: Evaluate the effects (and reallocate)

Step 1: Find and Screen Potential Items to Eliminate

You already have your vision and BAM. In other words, you can see both the business you're running and the life you want it to support. You've also marked potential elimination candidates on your BAM with an "E." Now it's time to formalize what gets cut.

Start with one question:

Does this move me measurably toward my vision?

There are only three answers: no, maybe, and yes.

If "No":

Cut it. There's no reason to keep it. You'd be better off reallocating those resources (time, energy, attention, money) to a more fruitful part of your business.

If "Maybe" or "Yes":

Screen further using these filters:

- Is this the *best* return on my resources?
- If I were starting from scratch today, would I include this?
- Will eliminating this help us ___? (Serve the mission better? Reduce stress and complexity? Save time or make money? Reduce mistakes and confusion?)

If the answer to any of those is "no," then they're going on the list to eliminate.

But before you start hacking away, do one last thing: run a quick pre-mortem. Look at both the obvious (direct) effects and the not-so-obvious (indirect/downstream/ripple) effects, both good and bad. This helps minimize the chance of regret, mistakes, and surprises.

There are four possibilities to examine (see Figure 13.1):

1. Positive Direct Effects
2. Positive Indirect Effects
3. Negative Direct Effects
4. Negative Indirect Effects

THE FOUR-EFFECTS MATRIX

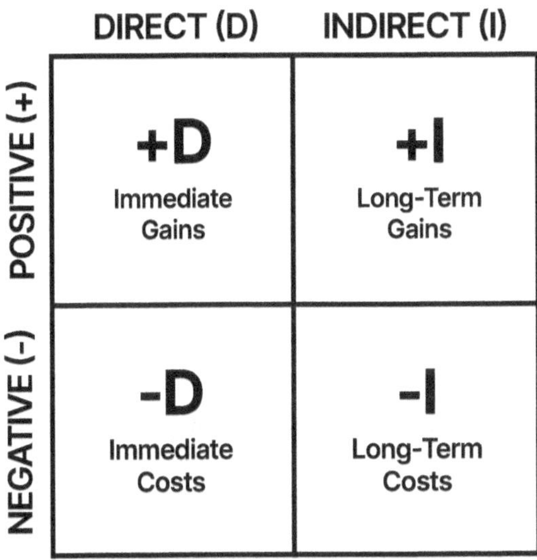

Figure 13.1: *Before making an elimination decision, check all four quadrants of the matrix. Not all consequences are immediate or obvious.*

Example: Eliminating a low-margin product line

1. **Positive Direct Effect:** You cut the product, and instantly free up $10,000/month in overhead tied to staffing, production, and storage.

2. **Positive Indirect Effect:** Your team shifts their energy into a higher-margin offering. This results in improved customer satisfaction and boosts overall profits within six months.

3. **Negative Direct Effect:** You lose $6,000/month in revenue from customers who were still buying the product.

4. **Negative Indirect Effect:** A few long-term customers who loved that product feel frustrated and decide to stop buying from you altogether. You also miss out on potential referrals they might have sent over.

Note that the goal isn't to avoid all negative outcomes. It's to weigh the pros and cons and make sure the end result is a net positive. In many cases, negative effects are unavoidable, and you just need to decide whether you can accept those consequences.

If you eliminate a product and lose some income in the short-term, is that OK with you? Or what if part of your business needs to be shut down, but your best friend since grade school is running it, and they're not interested in changing roles?

Still on the fence as to whether something should go? If possible, run a temporary (30–90-day) pause as a test instead of making a permanent cut. After you're done, check the four quadrants again and make a decision.

Lastly, I strongly advise that you involve your team in this process. Don't perform this step alone. Not only will they likely catch things that you're missing, but it's important to get their buy-in and support. This helps a ton in getting everyone aligned and reducing any resistance or discomfort they may feel.

People can be very fearful of change, so the more they know and contribute, the smoother the process will go. Talk through your rationale and thinking. Share your goals. Ask for their feedback, thoughts, and ideas. Explain why this is important, how it will make their life easier, and how it will benefit the business.

Step 2: Eliminate the Item(s)

With your list in hand, you're ready to start slicing and dicing. Start at the highest levels of the business, and work your way down. Think big rocks first. Removing a whole branch has a bigger impact than removing a single role, and cutting a single role beats cutting one responsibility.

As you move items into the queue for elimination, it's important to openly and regularly communicate the changes to employees and customers in advance. This reduces confusion and keeps trust intact.

Step 3: Evaluate the Effects (and Reallocate)

Once you've eliminated the item, you're not quite done yet. The next step is to monitor and evaluate the effects of that elimination. Are you seeing the benefits you expected? Has it increased alignment with your vision?

Some results, like lowering expenses, are immediate. Others may take time to reveal themselves (things like customer reactions after dropping a product line).

If negative unintended consequences pop up, don't panic. Many elimination decisions can be undone or modified if necessary. Sometimes it's just a matter of adjusting timing, communication, or scope.

Now comes the fun part: reallocation. Once you've said adios to the underperformers, you free up resources to put into higher-value areas.

WHEN ELIMINATION ISN'T THE ANSWER

It's important to note that sometimes what looks like it should be eliminated is actually a fixable problem in disguise. Yes, you should run every decision through the four possible effects I mentioned earlier (direct/indirect/good/bad), but there's one more question to consider before you axe something: *Why isn't this working?*

Asking this will help ensure you don't cut something prematurely. For example, imagine you have a product collecting dust on the shelf in retail stores. From what you've read thus far, you might just think: *It's not selling. Let's cut it.* But to truly make the best decision, you need to find out why it's not selling.

- Is the marketing off?
- Did the packaging change?
- Did the retailer move it to the bottom shelf?
- Are poor reviews scaring people off?

If the root cause is fixable, eliminating the product might be a mistake. This means instead of just having two options (keep or cut), you now have three: fix it, nix it, or keep it.

And even if it *is* fixable, you still need to ask whether the juice is worth the squeeze. Could the time, money, and energy required to fix the problem deliver a better return if applied somewhere else, perhaps to something that's already working well?

TOP FIVE ELIMINATION MISTAKES TO AVOID

You now know how powerful eliminating can be. But even with that knowledge, many entrepreneurs still stumble when it comes to implementation. Here are five of the most common mistakes to avoid if you want to eliminate with clarity and confidence:

Elimination Mistake #1: Waiting Too Long

Way too many owners get buried in the day-to-day of business and never step back to see the big picture. Over time, things pile up until the company becomes a confusing, clunky, slow-moving, bolted-together Frankenstein business. Schedule time, early and often, to elevate yourself above the business to see what might need to go. You can't cut the grass if you're stuck in the weeds.

Elimination Mistake #2: Letting Fear Drive the Bus

Fear whispers, *What if I need this later? What will people think if I cut this? What if I make a mistake?* Fear keeps you clinging to dead weight like that gym membership you haven't used in six years. Fear of failure, letting people down, judgment, and missing out, all surface as you consider eliminating. Just see fear for what it is, and move forward anyway.

Elimination Mistake #3: Shuffling Instead of Cutting

Sometimes (for whatever reason), you aren't quite ready to let something go. So instead of cutting it, you try to automate or delegate it. The problem is that now you've wasted valuable resources on something that shouldn't even be there. It's like taking the trash from your kitchen to your closet instead of putting it out on the curb.

Elimination Mistake #4: Ignoring the Data

Gut feelings and intuition have their place, but they're not a reliable method for eliminating things. Data should be your go-to tool for this process. That data can come from your vision, BAM, and metrics. Using data will keep you objective and allow you to make smarter, unbiased decisions, which will result in the best outcomes.

Elimination Mistake #5: Not Developing a Rhythm

Elimination isn't a one-time task. It's a recurring discipline that must be built into your normal business activities. Schedule and honor that time to keep the business slim and running smoothly. It's like taking a shower: doing it once is better than not at all, but once a month isn't going to cut it.

KEY TAKEAWAYS

1. Eliminating Comes First

Before thinking about automating or delegating, ask: *Does this even belong in my business?* Getting rid of something is the fastest, easiest, and most cost-effective way to simplify your business and maximize resources.

2. Nothing is Sacred

No area is off limits from being eliminated. This includes, but is not limited to: products, services, processes, tools, team roles, marketing efforts, or even clients. It's survival of the fittest, and everything is on the table. Use data to judge what stays and goes based on its contribution.

3. Keep the Best and Cut the Rest

By eliminating all but the best, most impactful parts of your business, you'll be able to concentrate your finite resources—time, focus, attention, and money—where they'll be most effective. Remove all the MUD (meaningless, unnecessary, or distracting) so that only the most valuable parts remain.

4. Simplicity Wins

A simple business is more profitable, resilient, easier to scale, and easier to run. Inside the company, this means your team will be better aligned, more focused, and more effective. And from the view of your customers, your branding, customer trust, and market positioning are all enhanced.

5. Master the Emotional Game

Fear of loss, sunk costs, FOMO, and shiny objects can sabotage your efforts to eliminate. Recognize those emotions for what they are, and don't let them stop you from doing what's best for the business and your vision.

PART V

SEAD: A FOR AUTOMATE

"Automation is good, so long as you know exactly where to put the machine."

—Eliyahu Goldratt

have a nerdy confession to make: I love business automation. In fact, don't tell this to elimination or delegation, but automation is my favorite of the three. I enjoy the thought process, strategy, and design, but most of all I enjoy the impact it has on my business.

But this wasn't always the case. I actually avoided automation for quite some time.

Several years ago, right after stepping in as CEO of Lifeonaire, I began analyzing the company, looking for areas to improve. When I reached our customer relationship management (CRM) software, I saw we were using one called Infusionsoft. I cringed because its nickname on the street was "Confusionsoft." People said it was overwhelming and had a steep learning curve.

When I asked the team about it, they confirmed my suspicions. Nobody really understood the capabilities of the software, and they were only using it for a few basic functions. I was ready to scrap it and pick something easier and cheaper, until I realized I couldn't make a fair comparison. I had no real idea what it could do, or how it would stack up against other options. Truth be told, I'd never even logged in myself because I was afraid I'd break something.

So, what did I do? Head over to YouTube. A few clicks later, I found a tutorial from a guy named Tyler Garns. He walked through how to build an automation, fully explaining each step. It was like the clouds parted and beams of sunlight bounced off my screen. For the first time, I started to see that automation was super learnable, incredibly powerful, and much less scary than I imagined. My very next thought was, *I'm an idiot for waiting so long to do this.*

I dove into automation headfirst, and the more I learned, the more I became obsessed. Fear and avoidance changed into excitement and wonder. I realized that automation, properly harnessed, was lightning in a bottle.

I started automating tasks, roles, and activities throughout the business. Internal processes. Customer-facing processes. Lead magnet delivery. Event registration. Member onboarding. One by one, as each automation was launched, we reduced workload, made fewer mistakes, and saved time.

Today, all the major parts of the company run on autopilot. Things are getting done in the background whether we're in the office, offsite teaching a live workshop, or on the beach.

And as proof this stuff works in real life, I had the honor of being awarded the prestigious iKON "Let's Grow" Business of the Year Award by Keap (the rebranded name for Infusionsoft). I don't share this to impress you, but to show you that if I can do this, you can too. The only difference is that you can skip the 100s of hours I've put in, and just piggyback on everything I've already figured out.

CHAPTER 14:
THE AUTOMATION ADVANTAGE

While automation can look complicated from the outside, the basic idea is very simple. Automation is just a canned response to something else that happens. Said another way, automation is a "when/then" response system. When something (X) happens, then the automation responds by doing something else (Y). Simple, right?

For example:

- *When* your prospect submits an inquiry form on your website, *then* automation triggers the appropriate action, whether that's to have them set up an appointment, deliver them key information, or alert a salesperson.
- *When* someone leaves you a positive review, *then* automation sends a thank you message and invites them to share a deeper testimonial.
- *When* a job applicant completes a step in the hiring process, *then* automation sends an email, prompting them to take the next step.

See? Not scary at all. And once these "little helpers" are working for you 24/7, you'll wonder how you ever lived without them.

Before we get into *how* to automate, I want to share a simple analogy to help you understand *why* it's so valuable.

Imagine a bucket, like one you'd bring to the beach. A good bucket has no holes. If you pour in water, it gradually fills up and eventually overflows. But if the bucket has any holes or cracks, then filling it is more difficult, if not impossible, because as the water is poured in, it continues to leak out.

Now imagine your business is that bucket. But instead of water, it's your resources (time, attention, energy, and money) being poured in. Eventually, if enough goes in, you produce the profits you desire. But if you have any holes or cracks—inefficiencies, gaps, or bottlenecks—it's unlikely you'll hit your goals.

Most entrepreneurs try to fix this by just pouring in more. More hours, more effort, more money. But that's the same as continuing to dump water into a cracked bucket. It's exhausting, wasteful, and unsustainable. The only way to fix the business long-term is to plug the holes. And automation is one of the best tools you'll ever use to do that.

Once you dive in and start automating, I have a hunch you'll feel the same way I do. Even if, like me, you're not a "tech person," automation can quickly become one of your favorite parts of the business. It's borderline magical. I'm hard-pressed to think of a business that wouldn't benefit from it, and frankly, I believe we're in an age where if you don't embrace automation, you'll eventually be outcompeted by those who do.

WHY DO WE AUTOMATE BEFORE WE DELEGATE?

We've already simplified by eliminating, and now it's time to amplify by automating. We do this before we delegate for a few key reasons:

First, automation is almost always cheaper than delegation. Things like salaries, benefits, and 401K matching don't apply to automation.

Not only that, there's nowhere on earth you can get someone to do what automation can in terms of volume, speed, and consistency, period.

According to Keap (the business automation software I mentioned earlier), their average user saves more than 40 hours per month by using automation. If you were doing all those tasks yourself, you just got a full workweek back, every single month. Imagine what you could do with that time. Or, think about the savings. If you're paying a team member $30 per hour to do those tasks, that's $1,200 per month. Automation software will run you a fraction of that amount.

Lastly, learning automation is easier than mastering delegation. Effective delegation has more moving parts: communication, training, follow-up, accountability, management skills, and more. Don't want to handle it yourself? No worries. It's still cheaper to pay someone to build and manage your automations than to bring on an experienced leader to run a team.

Let's break down exactly why automation is such a game-changer so that you see why it deserves your full attention.

Automation Benefit #1: Reduces Dropped Balls and Your To-Do List

If you're like most business owners, balls are being dropped every single day. Not because you don't care, but because you're stretched too thin. Everyone already has a thousand things on their schedule and a jam-packed to-do list, so important tasks get forgotten, postponed, or missed. This is where automation shines because every time something slips through the cracks, it costs you money.

If someone reaches out about your services and you don't follow up quickly, they may think, *"Geez, if this is how they treat me before they get my money, what's going to happen after I buy?"* You just lost the sale and hurt your reputation.

Or consider a new customer you ghost after they purchase because you got wrapped up with something else. Even if you didn't mean to, the impression you're leaving is *"I have your money, so you're no longer a priority."* That's not the message you want to give, and I know it's not your intention. It's just the result of doing too much.

If you were to pause and take inventory of all the things you frequently neglect, skip, or only give half the attention it requires, you might get a reality check on some changes that need to be made and where automation might help.

The number of items on your to-do list and the number of balls dropped are tightly correlated. Thankfully, automation reduces both. It can lighten your workload, fill the gaps, and prevent oversights.

Automation Benefit #2: Reduces Mistakes

Somewhat related to dropping balls is the issue of human error. Like it or not, we're all human, and humans make mistakes. We forget. We rush. We get distracted. Sometimes they're big, sometimes they're small, but in either case, they cost you in three ways:

1. You pay for the same job twice. Once the first time, and again to fix it.
2. You lose potential income. Time spent fixing the issue could have been spent generating new revenue.
3. Your credibility takes a hit. Every time you make a mistake, your reputation and competence are shaken, which can undermine staff morale and rob you of future business.

Automation reduces most of this risk. When set up correctly, it reduces human error by delivering the same result every single time. Not "60% of the time, it works every time," as Brian Fantana might say. It's every time. No slip ups, no cut corners, and no missed steps. No human on earth can match that level of consistency.

Automation Benefit #3: Maximizes Limited Resources

Many tasks simply shouldn't be done by people at all. Automation can do them faster, cheaper, and better. In addition, when you automate, you're freeing up your (and your team's) time for the activities that truly drive growth.

Back when I was a scientist in the lab, one of my least favorite tasks was doing experiments (kind of a problem, right?). While I loved thinking and talking about science, I found running experiments to be painfully boring and repetitive. I was pipetting chemicals, setting up machines, and following the same procedures over and over. It felt like such a waste of time and brainpower. It didn't make sense to me why someone trained to think, innovate, and solve complex problems should be stuck doing tasks a robot, or heck, even a teenager could do.

This applies to business as well. If you're stuck sending invoices, following up on missed payments, or manually entering leads into your CRM, you're basically doing "test tube work" instead of moving your company forward.

And even if your team is filled with rockstars who rarely miss things, you're still losing because you're overpaying *and* not spending enough time on the MVP or HBU tasks requiring a human touch.

Automation Benefit #4: Improves Customer Experience

Many people think automation feels cold or robotic, but that's only when it's done poorly. Repeating yourself over and over to a customer service phone bot or doing a Simon-says finger tap dance to get a live person on the phone…yeah, that's automation done wrong.

When customer-facing automation is done well, it should feel *more* personal. It should deliver the right message, at the right time, using your tone and personality. This leads to a better a customer experience, which improves, not hurts, your chances for more business.

For example, consider the onboarding of a new client:

- Their welcome email lands instantly and reliably. You look professional and on top of things.
- Check-ins are automatically scheduled so they occur at perfect intervals. This makes every client feel important and attended to.
- Ongoing educational content is delivered at the exact moment they need it. This nurtures the relationship and keeps you front of mind for future services.

All this…without lifting a finger.

Now, listen…Would it be better if you could personally send every email, text, and follow-up? Sure. But is this remotely possible at scale? Not a chance. A well-written, automated email from "you" (the automated version of you), beats no message every single time.

While we're at it, let's dispel another myth about automation: that it's very rigid and "one-size-fits-all." This is simply not true. It can respond based on behavior, tailor messages specific to the individual, and customize actions so every customer gets what they need.

Automation allows customers and prospects to feel good about doing business with you because they get personalized, attentive, consistent service—all of which help build engagement, loyalty, and referrals over time.

Automation Benefit #5: Provides a Solid Business Framework

Automation isn't just about saving time; it's about adding stability to your business. Regardless of what's going on in the marketplace, in your office, or in the lives of your team, automation is your guardian angel that will keep things rolling along. In this way, automation is the best business insurance you'll ever get.

Greg Jenkins, an automation expert, once said, "Think of automation as your star employee." It does exactly what you ask, as often as you ask, without rolling its eyes at you. It shows up for work every day, never gets tired, never complains, never forgets, and never quits.

People, on the other hand, get sick, take vacations, raise families, have off days, and sometimes move on. That's not bad, it's a normal part of life. But it does introduce instability into the business. Automation counterbalances that instability by providing consistency, precision, and reliability.

Please don't misunderstand. I'm not saying avoid working with people or don't have a team. Working with others is one of the most enjoyable and rewarding parts of business. What I am saying, is that automation steadies the ship when the seas are rough, and that support can help you sleep better at night.

Automation Benefit #6: Generates Infinitely Compounding Returns

The best types of investments are the ones you make once, and then continue to pay dividends forever without any additional work. Very few examples of these exist in real life. Imagine buying a rental property, only having to find a tenant once, never having to fix a single toilet, and still collecting rent month after month. How great would that be? Or how about going to the gym once and being in shape for life?! Sign me up!

Well, that's what automation is like. You set it up once, and it pays you back over and over again, for as long as you let it run. Said a different way, it provides an infinite return. Think of it like a flywheel. In the beginning it takes some effort to set up, but once it's in motion, it builds momentum. When your business is small, automation might only save you a few hours per week. But as your business grows and those automations run more and more often, those saved hours can become days or even weeks.

This is what makes automation the perfect tool for scaling. It doesn't care if it runs fifty times or fifty thousand. It never burns out or slows down, and there's no limit to volume or frequency. In contrast, scaling that relies on adding more people adds considerable complexity and expense.

While eliminating can streamline the business, and delegation adds human capacity, only automation gives you this type of compounding leverage. It's the closest thing to a perpetual motion machine your business will ever have.

CHAPTER 15:
WHAT TO AUTOMATE

By now, your mind might be racing with possibilities for what you can finally get off your plate. If so, that's awesome. If not, don't sweat it. Automation isn't second nature to most business owners, simply because we're so used to doing things ourselves or having other people do them, rather than relying on technology. It's a learning process. Even now, years into using automation, I still get fresh ideas and spot opportunities that I'd never thought of before.

So where do you begin? Here are three simple criteria for spotting strong automation candidates:

1. It is performed frequently in the business.
2. It is done the same way every time.
3. It does not require human interaction to complete.

Stated simply; **if a person is doing the same task repeatedly, the same way, again and again, then it's a strong candidate for automation.**

In real life, these are usually the boring, monotonous, joy-draining tasks that quietly eat up your time and energy, which means that automation doesn't just make your business more efficient; it also makes it more enjoyable. :)

On the other hand, if a task isn't performed very often, isn't done consistently, or requires human interaction, it's probably not a great fit for full automation (although parts of the process might be aided by automation).

Let's dive deeper into each of these three criteria so you can start recognizing automation opportunities in your business.

1. Tasks Performed Frequently

You may be wondering what "performed frequently" means. As a general guideline, if a task is a normal, recurring part of your business done at least a few times a week, it's a prime automation candidate. That said, this isn't a hard rule. A task performed less often might still be worth automating, as long as the return justifies the investment in the setup. One-off or rare situations aren't usually worth the effort. When it comes to automation, high volume equals high payoff.

2. Tasks Done Consistently

The best automation candidates are those done the same (or relatively the same) way each time. For example:

- You onboard new clients the same way each time.
- You always send a receipt after completing a service.
- You send the same welcome email or text when someone joins your mailing list.

While automation is much more flexible and customizable than you might think, it's best to keep it simple, especially in the early stages. As your confidence and skills grow, you can absolutely build more nuanced or sophisticated automations, but in many cases, I've seen simple, straightforward automations work beautifully.

3. Tasks That Don't Require Human Interaction

The best automation candidates require zero judgment, empathy, or creativity. These may be things that, until now, you've delegated to a team member, but automation is a step better. It doesn't just take things off your plate; it takes them off everyone's plate, permanently.

Of the three criteria, this one can be the trickiest to evaluate if you're not yet familiar with what automation can do. Many business owners underestimate just how much work can be shifted from staff to systems.

Having said that, not everything is a good fit for automation. Some tasks just require the human touch: coaching and mentorship, creative work, sales conversations, conflict resolution, negotiations, or handling sensitive customer service issues. And while automation can support these efforts, it should never replace them. (Even as AI continues to evolve, there are areas where a human connection will always matter.)

Lastly, realize that even when a task isn't a perfect fit for automation, parts or steps of it may be. Many processes could benefit from a hybrid approach, where some steps are performed by people, and others by automation. In this way, you get the best of both worlds: your team handles the parts that need a real person, and automation handles the rest.

CHAPTER 16:
HOW TO AUTOMATE

Now that you understand the incredible horsepower automation can add to your business, you're ready to automate your first process. Well, almost ready.

Before you jump in, go back to your MAP with the three criteria we just covered and look for tasks that are (1) repetitive, (2) performed in the same way, and (3) don't require the human touch. The tasks that check all three boxes are your best automation candidates. Review every task you marked with an "A" to confirm it's still a good automation candidate, and scan the rest of the map for anything you may have missed that could also be automated. Depending on your business, you may only have a handful of these, or you may have dozens. Over time, you'll want to automate all of them, but don't try to do everything at once.

Here's my advice as you start: **prioritize by impact.** Begin with what delivers the best return on making money, saving time, or ideally, both. In a perfect world, this is also your Most Valuable Priority (MVP) (although not every MVP is a good fit for automation).

If you're stuck, here are some questions to guide you:

- Where am I losing the *most* money due to ineffective, inefficient, or non-existent processes?

- What's the *biggest* untapped opportunity that I'm missing right now?
- What is the *biggest* bottleneck holding me back?
- What, if automated, would have the *biggest* impact on my bottom line?

For example:

- Your customer onboarding is non-existent, so retention suffers and cancelations are increased. Fix it with automation.
- Your lead nurture is inconsistent and has gaps, so you're losing prospects and sales. Automate it ASAP.
- Invoices are going out too slowly, so receivables lag and cash flow gets squeezed. Add in automation.

Fix the biggest issue first, then move down the list to the next most valuable task. Each win creates an automation snowball: you plug one leak, free up resources, then use those freed-up resources to fix the next leak. In this way, you build momentum and your efforts compound over time. Keep going until you've plugged all the holes that automation can fill.

One final note to consider before you go automation six-slinging: while you'll likely start with the direct, income-generating activities, don't overlook the non-income generating tasks. In many cases, it's the background admin work that eats up your bandwidth and prevents you and your team from focusing higher-value activities. Automating these "time vampires" can be just as valuable because they free you up for your HBU activities.

AUTOMATION PRINCIPLES

Through my own experience (*ahem*, mistakes) and learning from other experts, I've discovered a few practical yet powerful principles that will shorten your learning curve and make automation far less intimidating.

Automation Principle #1: Characterize and Simplify the Process Before You Automate It

To build a smooth, reliable automation, the underlying process you're automating must first be smooth and reliable. That might seem obvious, but remember: automation is an amplifier. You're adding gasoline to a fire. If your current process is clunky, confusing, or chaotic, automating it will turn a small mess into a giant one. (Ask me how I know.)

This means you must spend time on the front end, before you automate, to work out the kinks, friction points, and speed bumps. Only after it provides consistent, predictable, reliable results when done manually should you pull the genie out of the lamp and automate it.

Automation Principle #2: Keep It Simple and Start Small

Once you get a glimpse of what automation can do, it's a bit like opening Pandora's Box. Suddenly, every idea feels automation-worthy and it's easy to get carried away. You may start imagining wild, custom automations with all the bells, whistles, whiz-bangs of a world-class carnival ride. But there's a trap: the more complex an automation is, the more likely it is to never launch, or at the very least, take you much longer to build than it should.

Instead, just get the simple "Version 1" live. You can always expand, refine, and improve it later. You'll learn a whole lot more, faster, by launching something small and seeing how it does than by dreaming up something massive and never finishing.

Automation Principle #3: Work on, Complete, and Test One Automation at a Time

When I first discovered automation, I went a little crazy. I saw automation opportunities everywhere: sales, marketing, onboarding, billing, you name it. What did I do? I tried to automate them all at once. Not smart. All I had to show for all my hard work was a dozen half-finished automations. None launched. None making me money. And none saving me time.

Don't make the same mistake. Put that entrepreneurial ADD away and pick *one* automation to focus on at a time. Work on it until it's 100% complete, tested, and live. Then, and only then, move on to the next. Think of your automations like bridges. A bunch of half-built bridges won't take you anywhere. One finished bridge will though, and on the other side is more money, freedom, and peace of mind.

CHAPTER 17:
EXAMPLES OF AUTOMATION

L et's walk through some tasks and areas that can be automated so that you can begin to see just how wide the possibilities are. Some of these may not apply to your business, and that's ok. Note: this list only scratches the surface. For more ideas visit BusinessForLife.com.

SALES AND MARKETING AUTOMATION

Abandoned Cart Follow Up: When someone reaches your checkout page but doesn't buy, you're inches from a sale. The prospect may have gotten distracted, interrupted, or told themselves *"I'll come back later,"* but never do. Automated reminders (emails, texts, or retargeting ads) are a great way to nudge them back in a friendly, non-pushy way. Without automation, many of these near-sales are lost.

List-Building and Nurturing: Your email list is one of the most valuable assets in your business. It contains your customers, your future buyers, and your fans willing to give testimonials, reviews, and refer you to others. The larger and healthier your list, the more scalable and predictable your business becomes.

Automation is a powerhouse for managing and growing your list. Here are a few ways it can help you build and care for this resource:

- **Attracting and capturing new leads automatically.** Lead magnets like free reports, checklists, templates, and videos can be delivered instantly the moment someone opts-in. This is impossible manually.
- **Delivering customized, timely follow-up**. One-size-fits-all messaging is dead. Automation lets you send the right message at the right time based on the contact's behavior or interests, which makes your communication feel relevant, not generic.
- **Re-engaging cold or inactive contacts.** Contacts who haven't opened your emails in a while are less likely to buy from you and will eventually lose interest in your brand. Automation can send them a friendly "wake up" sequence to pull them back in and reignite interest in your services.
- **Cleaning your list.** Even the best lists get bombarded with fake contacts and spambots. Automation can identify and remove them so your list stays clean and healthy, which means better deliverability and higher open rates.

Sales Processes: There's an old saying in sales that "the fortune is in the follow-up," and it's true. Many prospects require time, repeated touches, and gentle reminders before they're ready to buy. That's why you need to follow-up consistently and stay front-of-mind.

Most sources claim it takes 7–12 touchpoints for a prospect to convert into a customer, and that number is only rising. Multiply that across hundreds or thousands of prospects, and you'll quickly understand why manual follow-up is impossible and automation is your only option.

Automation helps ensure that leads don't slip through the cracks and increases the probability of buying. It can provide strategic and timely communications to overcome objections and build trust. Done right, it's like having a tireless sales rep working behind the scenes, making sure every warm lead stays warm until it's time to buy.

Reviews, Ratings, and Testimonials: The importance of positive reviews and ratings cannot be overstated. What's the first thing you look at when considering an Amazon purchase? The star rating and the number of people who left the rating. That's why collecting and sharing positive reviews, ratings, and testimonials from satisfied customers isn't just nice, it's vital.

The challenge is that most business owners struggle to get them consistently. It feels awkward, or it gets lost in the busyness of running the business. Automation fixes this in a snap.

Automation can request reviews at the perfect time (right after a great experience). And if for some reason a customer is unhappy, automation can catch that too. This means you have a chance to turn that frustrated customer into a raving fan.

OPERATIONS AND ADMINISTRATION

Appointment Scheduling: If you're still going back and forth trying to find a meeting time, stop. It's inefficient and makes you look like an amateur. Automation allows you to share a booking link based on your availability and send reminders with pre-meeting information, which both reduce no shows and makes your business look more professional.

Billing, Invoicing, and Collections: Getting paid shouldn't be awkward or time consuming. Automation can generate and send invoices when a service is completed, run recurring payments, and even remind clients when their card on file is about to expire. Even better, automation can run multiple charge attempts and send polite messages to the cardholder if their card declines, cutting down on uncomfortable conversations. *Nice!!!*

The impact of all this is that you get paid faster, easier, and with less friction. Now, instead of micromanaging receivables, you can let automation handle it and focus on making more money.

CUSTOMER SERVICE SUPPORT

Strong customer service is one of the most critical pillars of a successful business. Fall short here and you'll have unhappy customers, lower retention, and get trashed online with poor reviews. On the other hand, do it well and you'll create supporters who will continue to do business with you and refer others.

The challenge is that great customer service requires a lot of attention, which is hard to maintain when your team is juggling dozens of other responsibilities. Have no fear though, because automation can be a powerful ally in making sure your customers have a world-class experience.

Automation can provide customized answers to FAQs, provide order tracking, and give self-service options, all without ever contacting your team.

Even cooler, like we discussed, automation can help customize a client's experience based on their actions.

- A customer buys a digital course but doesn't log in? Automation can send a series of friendly reminders and offer tips on getting started.
- A client registers for your live event? Automation can send them venue information, pre-event homework, and timely reminders.
- A prospect expresses interest in your services? Automation can deliver information tied to that interest.

The result is a personalized, professional, helpful experience tailored to their specific needs.

TEAM AND HR

Hiring Process Support: Selecting the right team members is critical, but it can also be incredibly overwhelming. Finding the time to sift through dozens or hundreds of résumés, conduct interviews, and communicate with applicants can be nearly impossible, at least without bringing the rest of the business to a screeching halt. This is where automation has got your back.

Automation can help you systematize the process while keeping it warm and professional. For example, automation can:

- Help filter applications using keywords or other criteria.
- Send updates to candidates so they don't feel left in the dark.
- Move applicants through steps and provide clear instructions.

You save hours, and your candidates feel valued and respected. And by the time you step in personally, you're only meeting with the most qualified candidates.

Employee Onboarding and Training: Bringing on a new team member is exciting. It represents growth, fresh energy, and new potential for the business. Yet it's also time-consuming and requires a lot of attention. Automation can help in carrying that load because so much of the onboarding and training process is repetitive. You probably walk every new hire through the exact same systems, steps, and instructions, and so automation can assist without sacrificing the personal touch.

For example, by delivering training videos, documents, and walk-throughs, you can provide a clear, consistent onboarding experience every single time. You can also set up interactive elements like short quizzes to assess understanding, and milestone awards to celebrate progress. And once they're up and running, automation can continue to support your team with templates, checklists, task reminders, and cheat sheets to reduce mistakes and make their work easier.

The result? Your new hires feel confident and cared for, your managers save valuable time, and you free up more time for the human side of leadership: mentoring, coaching, and building relationships.

BRINGING IT ALL TOGETHER

As you can see, the possibilities and applications of automation are not only endless, but wildly powerful. Automation isn't just a "nice-to-have," it's the backbone of a modern business. It creates a stable scaffolding for your business that is simply impossible to replicate with human effort alone. Without automation, you're building a sandcastle more than you are a business.

In choosing a specific automation platform, do your own research to determine which best fits your needs and goals. There are several solid platforms out there. Yes, the automation software is important, but even more important is that you just start embracing the process of automation itself. Do that, and you'll look back and wonder how you ever ran your business without it.

TOP FIVE AUTOMATION MISTAKES

Automation is incredible when used correctly, but there's a handful of landmines that could derail your progress if you're not careful. The good news is they're easy to avoid once you're aware of them. Here are the top five automation mistakes entrepreneurs make, and how to steer clear of them.

Automation Mistake #1: Avoiding Automation Out of Fear

Anything new can be daunting, and automation is no different. Technology in particular can be intimidating for many, but don't let that hold you back from the benefits it can unlock.

Think about it this way: the cockpit of an airplane is overwhelming to the non-pilot, yet those instruments are what make global travel possible. The neck of a guitar looks confusing to someone who's never played, but with practice, it can produce music that moves hearts. Automation works the same way. It might be scary to start, but once harnessed, it has the power to revolutionize your business.

And if I can be frank, whether you like it or not, technology will continue to play an increasingly larger role in our world, so you need to get comfortable with it now. Look around: factory workers have been replaced by robotics, front-line cashiers by self-serve kiosks, DVDs by digital streaming, and handheld cameras and GPS units by smartphones. Businesses that don't embrace technology will become extinct. Don't let that be you.

And yes, you will make mistakes. You're going to miss things. You're going to send an email to your entire list that says, "Put something smart and interesting here" in the email subject line because you forgot to take out the placeholder text (or maybe that's just me). Regardless, don't let it hold you back. Do it anyway. You're smart enough. You can make this work. And listen, if doing this yourself just isn't your thing, then hire someone else to handle it.

Automation Mistake #2: Automating Too Early

Automation is an amplifier. What this means is that if your process is smooth, clear, and effective, automation will put it on steroids. But if the process is clunky and duct-taped together, automation will create a disaster. Automation makes what's good better and what's bad worse.

Bill Gates nailed it when he said, "The first rule of any technology used in business is that automation applied to an efficient operation will magnify the efficiency. The second is that automation applied to an inefficient operation will magnify the inefficiency."

Like I mentioned earlier, automation can be your star employee because it executes flawlessly…but there's one downside: it can't think on its own. It only does exactly what you tell it, over and over. This is why you must first map out, clarify, and refine your process before you automate it. Otherwise, you'll just be multiplying the chaos.

A playful illustration of this comes from Disney's *The Sorcerer's Apprentice*. In the story, Mickey, tired of doing all the chores, steals the sorcerer's magic hat with the intent of using it to complete his work.

He casts a spell on his broom, which then grows arms and legs and starts filling, carrying, and pouring buckets of water for Mickey (one of his least favorite tasks). He jumps for joy, then decides to take a nap with his newfound freedom.

Everything is wonderful, until he is abruptly awoken by a splash of water in his face. He looks around and sees that the room is flooded. The broom had continued working while Mickey was sleeping. He feels a pit in his stomach when he realizes he doesn't know the magic words to stop the broom. He tries everything he can think of, but the broom continues without slowing down.

Mickey finally gets the idea to chop up the broom with an axe, which stops it for a moment, but then each splinter of wood grows into another broom. Before long, there's an unstoppable army of brooms drowning him in water.

Just when it appears all is lost, the sorcerer reappears, angrily casts a spell, and all the water and brooms disappear. All that remains is the single original broom, which Mickey grabs sheepishly and goes back to work.

That's what happens when you automate too early. Unless you know what you're doing and have the full process clarified from start to finish, it's not going to turn out the way you'd hoped. But when you do, automation works like magic.

Automation Mistake #3: Automating Too Late

The opposite mistake of automating too early (waiting too long) is just as costly. If you feel like you're working harder than ever, yet balls are being dropped left and right, then you've waited too long to automate. Feel like you're too busy to automate? You're the *exact* person who needs it most. Money shouldn't be an excuse either. You can't afford *not* to automate. The cost of automation is peanuts compared to the ROI. As I mentioned earlier, you'll never find anyone (even an overseas VA) who can do a fraction of what automation can do at anywhere close to the cost.

Lastly, if you already have more than a handful of team members on payroll, you've waited too long to automate. Once you have money to hire team members, you should also be spending money on automation. You're paying people to do tasks that software could handle for pennies on the dollar, and so you might even say it's irresponsible *not* to automate.

Automation Mistake #4: Becoming Consumed with Automation

In some ways, I think automation has the potential to be the "one ring" from the movie *Lord of the Rings* because its power and allure can be intoxicating. Speaking from experience, it's easy to go down the rabbit hole and spend more time thinking and tinkering than actually running your business.

At the end of the day, remember that automation is just a tool. Its purpose is to help you reach your business objectives, not to become a shiny distraction. Keep your enthusiasm in check and remember that success isn't measured by how many of the software features you're using, but rather how many of the right things in your business are automated.

Automation Mistake #5: Not Testing or Monitoring Your Automations

Once you've created your automation, you're not done. Before you go live, you must test, test, then test again. Even a small mistake can create expensive and embarrassing issues such as customers receiving the wrong emails, invoices failing to send, or steps firing out of order.

The other habit you need to develop is periodic monitoring after your automation goes live. As your skillset and "automation awareness" grows, you'll see areas you can improve or tweak. Also, as your business evolves, what was perfect six months ago may not be aligned today.

KEY TAKEAWAYS

1. Business Automation Is a Game-Changer

Automation is a powerful tool that boosts efficiency, reduces mistakes, and saves time. By taking repetitive, tasks off your plate, it frees you and your team to focus on higher-value, growth-driving work. Whether leveraged for marketing, sales, operations, or customer service, automation strengthens both the internal engine of your business and the external experience for your customers.

2. Automate Before You Delegate

Delegation is valuable, but automation should come first because it's cheaper, faster, and more consistent when it comes to repetitive tasks. Automation is a cost-effective way to build a "business machine" that keeps work moving along 24/7, without fatigue, delays, or human error.

3. Prioritize Automation for Maximum Results

Not all tasks are created equal. Start with the highest-impact, most important areas in your business and work your way down. Once you plug the holes that are costing the most money and/or time, gradually expand to the other less impactful areas.

4. Keep It Simple

Automation tends to evolve and become more complex over time as your skill level increases. Resist the urge to over-engineer and always prioritize simplicity in your automation. Done and running smoothly beats perfect but unfinished every single time.

5. Compounding Returns

The real magic of automation lies in its compounding effect. Every process you automate will continue to pay dividends long after the initial setup. This shows up as saved time, stronger profits, and improved scalability. And over time, these small, ongoing wins snowball into massive growth.

PART VI

SEAD: D FOR DELEGATION

*"No person will make a great business who wants to do it all himself
or get all the credit."*

—Andrew Carnegie

After finishing high school, Josh made a bold decision: instead of following the traditional path of going to college, he set off to explore the world. For four years, he backpacked across China, wandered through Europe, and even lived in Australia for a year. He fell in love with the adventure of travel, the beauty of new cultures, and the excitement of meeting people from every corner of the globe.

But alas, eventually the money started to run out, and the nagging question, "*What am I going to be when I grow up?*" forced him to hit pause. He knew he needed a career, but it couldn't be just any career. It had to give him the flexibility, income, and freedom to scratch his travel itch. He got the idea that owning apartments might be his golden ticket, and so he took a job working for a local multifamily investor to learn the ropes.

He quickly fell in love with providing quality housing, but also discovered that the business demands were relentless. Sixty-hour work-weeks quickly became the norm. Travel was out of the question, and even a normal life outside of work became impossible.

Josh realized the only way to reclaim his freedom was to run his own business, and when the opportunity came, he seized it. He quit his job, and he and his wife Kayla bought their first multifamily apartment. It was game on. They rolled up their sleeves and went to work, doing every-thing themselves. They handled showings, leases, collections, mowing the lawn, even shoveling snow.

But they weren't prepared for what happened next. Because they were so good at what they did, business boomed. More and more prop-erties continued to be added to their portfolio, and they became victims of their own success. And while they'd hired a few team members, with every new property acquisition, the workload, complexity, and chaos multiplied, preventing them from being able to step back and relax. Josh realized that if he was going to ever be able to travel again, he'd need to change how he ran the company.

The first place he looked was himself. Up until that point, he admits he'd been winging it as a leader. He was disorganized, inconsistent, and not the person his team members needed him to be. The result was stress, confusion, and friction in the company. He had also backed himself into a corner as the "go-to guy" for every decision and problem, creating a huge bottleneck in the business.

He realized that if he wanted to create freedom, he had to mature into a better leader and business owner. He needed to build a *real* business with the right people, solid systems, and clear processes in place. He went to work. He created a detailed org chart and documented clear standard operating procedures. He put together a hiring, onboarding, and training system. He started pouring into his people and developing them as leaders. Piece by piece, Josh built a business that could function without him.

It wasn't an overnight success and it wasn't easy, but steadily, the business improved. It became more organized, more efficient, and self-sustaining. Josh was finally able to step down as CEO (chief everything officer) and start living the life he originally dreamed of.

Today, Josh and Kayla own more than 800 units and lead a team of over 50 people. They work about 10 hours per week (20 on the occasional "heavy" week), and spend four to six months each year traveling the world. Their longest trip so far lasted three months straight. All this, while the business continues running smoothly in the background. As a matter of fact, at the time of writing of this book, they'd bought a one-way ticket to Europe with no set return date. They'll come back when they feel like it. No timeline. No restrictions or deadlines.

That's the payoff and power of setting up your business the right way.

CHAPTER 18:
THE DELEGATION MINDSET

I was sitting in Clate Mask's office at the Keap headquarters in Chandler, Arizona. I had recently won their *"Let's Grow" iKON Business of the Year* award, and was invited to speak at their annual company kickoff.

Clate is the cofounder and former CEO of Keap, the world's leading business-automation platform for companies in the $1M to $10M range. We were discussing delegation and leadership, and when you're talking with someone who took a three-person company earning a couple grand per month into a 300+ employee, nine-figure powerhouse at the forefront of its industry, you listen.

"The key to growing a company," he told me, "is breaking off pieces of yourself and giving them to someone else, over and over again."

He continued, "Being a business owner is an exercise in relinquishing control. In the beginning, you do everything, and that's fine. But if you want to grow, you have to evolve. You must continually evaluate your roles, break off the least valuable pieces, and hand them to others. That's the only way to move forward."

That conversation changed how I view business. I had never seen the irony so clearly: the very things that help you get off the ground are the same things that cap your growth later. It's just like flying an airplane. The wing flap and throttle settings that get you off the runway aren't the same ones that will keep you in the air. The same goes for business. As you climb (grow), everything must adjust: your focus, systems, and skills. Otherwise, you'll stall out and maybe even crash.

When done right, the payoff from delegation is massive. You reclaim your time and can focus on high-impact activities. Your company gains new skillsets, experience, and expertise. Problems get solved without you. And the business expands beyond your personal bandwidth.

No matter how much, or how well you eliminate and automate, you still need human help. Even the best systems and processes still require people to execute them, and while AI is powerful, it can't (yet) replace a living, breathing person in all ways.

That's why mastering the art and science of delegation is a nonnegotiable, and it all starts with having the right mindset.

EMBRACING THE DELEGATION MINDSET

I've worked with business owners all over the world, and I hear the same objections to delegation. If I had a dollar for every time someone told me, "You can't trust anyone," or "No one wants to work hard," or "I can do it quicker myself," I'd give Warren Buffett a run for his money.

And while there may be a grain of truth in these complaints, if you want to be successful, you have to see them for what they really are: damaging beliefs that will sabotage your ability to grow a team and build a real business. If you cringe at the thought of hiring or delegating, your results will reflect that mindset. It will become a self-fulfilling cycle. But if you can shift your view and see the benefits of working with people, then you have taken the first step toward effective leadership.

Now to be clear, I'm not saying working with people is always unicorns and rainbows. Most business owners, myself included, have been burned. Everyone has a horror story, or ten, about a hire gone wrong. Maybe you had to fire someone who couldn't show up on time, missed deadlines, or even stole from you. Maybe someone quit without any advanced notice, and you were left holding the bag. I've dealt with all of those—more than once. But you can't throw in the towel. You can only do things better next time.

Along these lines, if you're open to it, there's another perspective that might change how you view your bad experiences. It might feel harsh, unfair, or flat-out untrue, but it's incredibly empowering. It's this:

Any time something goes wrong with a team member, look for where you share responsibility. And if you're willing to take it a step further, assume it was your fault. Yes, you read that right. Blame yourself.

Once you're done cursing me out in your head (or maybe even out loud), hear me out. When you take ownership of a negative experience, it opens the door to growth. It forces you to examine what happened, learn the lesson, and improve for the next time, *and yes, there will be a next time.* The alternative of deciding "people suck" only keeps you stuck as an overworked, burned-out entrepreneur with a business that's smaller and more stressful than it should be.

And to be clear, "taking responsibility" isn't code for *secretly blaming them but pretending to be noble about it.* I mean *really* looking at where you contributed to the problem.

Think back to your worst hiring experience:

Was the person screened properly…or did you rush?

Did you onboard and train them effectively…or did you wing it?

Did you set clear expectations and priorities…or gloss over things?

You get the point. Often, the honest answer reveals that you played a role too. I'm sharing this because maybe, just maybe, delegation isn't as bad as you think. You just have to address a few things and get better at it.

Are we still friends? Cool.

Hopefully this helps you shift your mindset, because it matters more than you might think. Your perspective leaks into your behavior, which shapes your company culture. If you're jaded from previous trauma and carry that baggage, candidates and team members will sense it. You'll repel the A-players and attract people who mirror your poor attitude. And if by some miracle a superstar joins the team, they won't stay long. No talented, high-level performer wants to work for a cynical, bitter boss. That's why changing our perspective is step one. Effective delegation begins long before you ever hand off a task; it starts with how you think about people.

THE USUAL SUSPECTS

Let's look at some of the most common reasons (*cough…excuses*) business owners use to avoid hiring, so we can dismantle them and move forward with building the team you need.

"NOBODY CARES ABOUT MY BUSINESS LIKE I DO"

You're right, and that's OK. But that doesn't stop someone from doing excellent work. Your employees may not love your business the way you do, but my guess is they *do* want a steady paycheck, meaningful work, and a stable, enjoyable environment.

And frankly, you *should* be the one who cares the most. Unless your team members have equity or profit-sharing, why would they be as invested as you? That's like expecting the babysitter to love your kids as much as you do.

Some owners even say, "This is my baby." And that's fine…but just like a child needs to grow into a fully-functional, capable adult, your business should mature into a company that doesn't require you for its daily survival.

Can it be hard when your kid heads off to college? Sure (depending on which kid, right?). But the alternative is having a 35-year-old, unemployed "child" living in your basement while you still cook and do their laundry. I'm guessing that's not the result you're looking for, so don't do the same thing to your business.

"NO ONE CAN DO IT AS GOOD AS ME"

Let's be real…if this is your belief, the reason is usually pride, ignorance, or being too cheap to hire good help. Unless you're truly a sparkling, one-of-a-kind unicorn (spoiler: you're probably not), there are plenty of people out there who can not only match your skill but might even make you look like an amateur. Ask me how I know. Thinking you're the only one capable of doing something exceptionally is your ego combined with a lack of exposure to top-tier talent.

But let's play devil's advocate for a moment. Say you really are the best in the world at what you do. Is that the *only* thing on your plate as the business owner? Of course not. You're juggling dozens of other responsibilities. And just like the world's best juggler can only keep so many balls in the air before dropping one, the same applies to you. It doesn't matter if you're extremely capable. You're still just one person.

Here's some math to back this up: if you're theoretically operating at 100% skill level for a task, but can only give it 20% of your time, then someone with 80% of your skill who can give 100% of their time is the smarter choice by a factor of four. Skill isn't the only variable; focus matters too.

And lastly, don't forget—you probably weren't great when you started either. You learned, you stumbled, and got better. Why not allow your team members that same process? With the right training and support, they'll grow quickly, and in time, may even surpass you (and that's a good thing!).

"IT'S QUICKER FOR ME TO JUST DO IT MYSELF"

This statement is true the first time you perform a task. But what about the 10th or 100th? If you break past this short-term mindset and expand the time horizon, you'll see that it's always faster to train your replacement.

Yes, this takes longer upfront, but the payoff compounds over time.

For example: A task takes you five minutes. Training someone would take thirty. That means you're "in the red" for the first five repetitions, break even at the sixth, and from then on, you're ahead. Multiply that across the dozens of recurring tasks in your business, and it becomes pretty clear how it's worth the investment to train someone.

"I CAN'T AFFORD TO PAY SOMEONE"

Money fears stop more business owners from hiring than almost anything else, so let's examine this concern from a few different angles.

First, is how you view your team members. If you look at your team as a cost, you'll struggle and stay stuck. If you see them as an investment, you'll grow and be poised for success.

Investments require time, money, and attention to generate a return, and team members are no different. When you choose wisely, train them correctly, and lead them well, your payoff shows up as a better business and more time for you.

Also realize that every team member should pay for themselves, either directly or indirectly. Sales roles contribute to revenue by bringing in more money, and admin roles contribute by freeing up your bandwidth. If you hire someone for $20/hour and that allows you to focus on $200/hour work, you just made a 10x return. Not too shabby.

And lastly, if finances really are that tight, you can start by hiring someone part-time based on your budget. Even five to ten hours per week of extra help can be a game-changer. They don't have to be a full-time commitment.

"I'LL MAKE LESS MONEY IF I HIRE PEOPLE"

This belief is a close cousin of "I can't afford to pay someone." And just like that one, it doesn't hold up. Hiring people should make you *more* money, not less. A good hire gets things done that are currently being neglected. When those issues get fixed, revenue increases.

But let's say you *do* make less profit. Would it still be worth it? What if you're less stressed and overwhelmed because now you have help? What if your marriage improves because you're no longer working late every night? Remember, profit isn't the only metric of success. Sometimes buying back your time and peace of mind is the biggest win of all.

"I'LL LOSE MY IDENTITY"

If you've pushed past the other excuses for not hiring others, congratulations. But there's a deeper one that still might be lurking: delegation can feel like a threat to your identity. You won't say this out loud, but you'll feel it internally. We covered the idea of identity earlier in explaining why we work so much, but it's worth mentioning here because it may cause you to struggle with delegation.

You're good at what you do. You've built a reputation as being the hard worker, the problem-solver, and the one who keeps all the plates spinning. You're the hero who saves the day, and you're used to the praise and recognition that comes with that.

But what happens when you're no longer needed in that role because you have people, systems, and processes in place? For a lot of entrepreneurs, that question is terrifying. Who are you if you're not the linchpin holding it all together? Where do you fit now?

This fear is compounded when your need for recognition, competence, or significance isn't being met outside of work. (Again, this is why you need a vision. You must design a life that meets those needs in healthy ways.) The result is that you sabotage the business by white-knuckling your roles and refusing to bring on help, despite the rising costs to your life and sanity.

The irony is that as a business owner, your ultimate goal *should* be to make yourself replaceable. If you can "fire yourself" and the business keeps humming along, that's a win. That's the freedom we're after. So, the question you need to ask yourself is this: Do you want to keep being the hero who saves the day…or do you want to build a business that doesn't need saving?

CHAPTER 19:
BEYOND DELEGATION

Delegation, by definition, is simply the act of handing off work to another person. Easy enough, right? Not quite. There are *a lot* of places that delegation can go wrong. That's why we're going to go deep, both strategically and tactically on delegation. But before we do, we need to address something most business owners tragically overlook: there are multiple steps involved in successful delegation. It's a process, not a pass-off. In order to be successful, you must learn how to find, attract, screen, hire, onboard, and train the right teammates. And that's before you even get to the delegation piece itself. Miss any one of those steps and you'll likely end up disappointed and frustrated with your new hire.

Another mistake owners make is assuming that because you're good at your craft, you're automatically good at all the steps I just mentioned. That's just not true. They're completely unrelated. These activities live in the world of HR, not your trade. The good news is these skills can be learned, and if you're willing to develop them, you'll unlock the true power of delegation.

With that out of the way, let's start with two key questions: Which position should you hire first, and what kind of person are you looking for?

WHAT POSITION TO HIRE FIRST

My philosophy on making your first hire is the same as with automation: **Find the biggest hole in your business and fill it.** Contrary to what others may say, there's no universal, one-size-fits-all answer that would be correct 100 percent of the time.

That being said, many times the smartest first hire is someone who can take the low-wage, low-value work off your plate that is unsuitable for automation. Think administrative, operational, or executive assistant type roles.

If you're doing everything yourself, this is a game-changer. With these tasks off your back, your attention can now be redirected toward the high-value, high-impact activities that make a difference. Their job is to free up your time, not replace your expertise.

Other early hires may include:

- Sales people or appointment setters, especially if they're commission-only because there's zero financial risk to the business.
- Specialists like a website developer, or graphic designer.

Again, remember to hire for the biggest return. As the business grows and has more resources, you'll be able to afford more experienced and more expensive hires. By then, you'll also have more experience hiring and leading, so you'll be less likely to make a costly mistake.

Now that you know which position to fill, let's talk about the type of person you should be looking for.

DEFINING YOUR PERFECT CANDIDATE

The first step to finding the right team member is knowing exactly who you're looking for. What are the traits, characteristics, and skills they should have—and just as importantly, which ones shouldn't they have? Trying to hire without this clarity is like going through a buffet line blindfolded. You'll walk away with something, but it probably won't be what you wanted.

There are two parts to this process. First, evaluate candidates through the lens of the 3Cs: character, capability, and culture. Then, get more specific by applying what I call the 4F Filter: a simple, four-category matrix that adds a deeper level of objectivity and granularity.

THE 3CS: YOUR FOUNDATION FOR EVERY HIRE

Regardless of the role, every great hire must be a match for you in three key areas: character, capability, and culture.

CHARACTER

This one should be obvious, yet it's often ignored. Avoid hiring anyone with questionable ethics, a poor attitude, or who displays undesirable behaviors, no matter how skilled or experienced they are.

Do your best to assess these traits using the screening tools we'll discuss shortly. Look for inconsistencies between what a candidate says, what they do, and what others say about them.

Consider placing character at the very top of your hiring criteria, even above skills, because it greatly impacts your company's culture and brand reputation. If you wouldn't trust them to house-sit while you're on vacation or watch your kids for a couple hours, I'd encourage you to think twice about hiring them.

CAPABILITY

Capability answers the question: "Can they do the job well?" This includes their skills, experience, knowledge, and even their time availability.

For entry-level positions, capability doesn't matter quite as much as it does for higher-level roles because the skills can be taught and developed fairly easily. But as you move into more specialized and advanced roles, a candidate's pre-existing capabilities become much more important.

CULTURE

Culture is the collective attitudes, beliefs, and behaviors of your team. It starts with you, and then spreads to the rest of the organization. This means you must personally model the culture you wish to have.

When hiring, you must gauge how well a candidate will integrate into your current culture (and improve it moving forward).

Ask:

- Are they optimistic and uplifting? Or critical and pessimistic?
- Do they show gratitude and appreciation? Or entitlement?
- Are they looking to give and contribute? Or get a free ride?
- Would you enjoy having person in your life? Or dread every interaction?

Culture isn't fluff. It's real, and it matters—a lot. A Super Bowl–winning team will always beat a Pro Bowl team because the former is unified and plays together as a team. The Pro Bowl squad, despite having better talent, isn't aligned as a unit.

Potential areas of cultural fit to consider:

- Communication style

- Alignment with your mission, values, and purpose
- Attitude toward learning and growth
- Ability to thrive as a team player
- Abundance vs. scarcity mindset
- Desired personality traits like optimism, positivity, and encouragement

The 3Cs give you a strong foundation for screening candidates. But we can get even more precise.

THE 4F FILTER: OBJECTIVITY'S BEST FRIEND

It can be really hard to objectively screen candidates. People are so different and complex, and there are so many variables to consider. How do you compare Ted, who's good with numbers, to Rusty, who is a bit friendlier?

Part of this difficulty stems from not knowing which traits are most important. No two applicants are identical, and so without a proper framework to measure these traits, emotion and subjectivity creeps in.

The solution is simple: Make a full list of every trait, characteristic, and skill you can think of for the role you're hiring. Write down everything. Then place each item into one of four categories of the 4F Filter. This simple classification system removes a lot of the guesswork, reduces bias, and gives you firm rules to guide your decisions.

The four categories are:

1. **Foundational (Non-negotiables):** These are your must-have traits, skills, or characteristics. Missing any of these means it's an automatic "no." These represent the core qualities someone must possess to succeed in the role.

2. **Favorable (Important):** These matter significantly, but there's a bit of flexibility. A candidate can be missing one or two, as long as other strengths compensate for it. Think of these as strong preferences rather than dealbreakers.

3. **Frosting (Nice-to-Haves):** These are the icing-on-the-cake. They make a great candidate even better, but they're not essential to the position's success. This category helps avoid the trap of overvaluing shiny qualities that don't impact performance.

4. **Fatal Flaws (Disqualifiers):** These are the hard nos. The traits or behaviors that are unacceptable and immediately rule someone out. No amount of skill, talent, or charm overrides a Fatal Flaw.

Using this filter gives you an objective hiring criterion and dramatically reduces bias. It also ensures you're evaluating every candidate the same way so that you're consistent across the board. What you write here will also provide the backbone of your job description, which is where we're headed next.

CREATING A GREAT JOB DESCRIPTION

Now that you've clarified exactly who you're looking for, the next step is to get their attention. This is where your job description comes in. This is one of the most important tools you have for attracting the right candidates. Just like you write sales copy to attract your ideal customers, you're now creating copy to attract future ideal team members. In many ways, your job description is your sales letter for talent, and time and effort spent here will pay dividends later. After reading it, your prospect should say to themselves, *"This is me!"*

Here's what every great job description should include:

- **Your company's mission, purpose, and vision.** Tell people what you stand for and what you're about, so they can self-select.
- **Why the role matters.** Paint the big picture. Show how this position is important to the success of the company and its mission.
- **Key responsibilities.** List the main tasks they'll be doing and what a typical day looks like.
- **Expectations of the position.** Define what "winning" is, how performance will be measured, and how they'll be held accountable.
- **Who the successful candidate will be.** Describe the traits, expertise, experience, and skills you're looking for. Also include who will *not* be a good fit.
- **A realistic glimpse of your culture.** Don't skip this. Give an honest view of what it's like to work with you. If everyone works 12-hour days, 7 days a week, don't claim work/life balance is a priority. If prayer before meetings is part of your culture, say it.

Again, don't skimp here. Also remember, your goal isn't to get the most applicants—it's to attract the right ones and repel the wrong ones. A clear, authentic job description helps you do that. Along those lines, let the tone of the posting itself match the personality of the company. If your team jokes around a lot, feel free to write that way. If your work environment is serious, then make your writeup more formal and professional.

I also strongly recommend including the pay range in the posting. Early in my hiring journey, I used to leave this out because I wanted people to buy into our mission first, not just apply for the paycheck. What happened was we wasted a lot of time with candidates whose income needs didn't match our pay scale.

If you'd like to see real job descriptions I've used successfully in the past, check out BusinessForLife.com.

Now that you have your job description, let's set our sights on finding your next rockstar team member.

CHAPTER 20:
FINDING YOUR SUPER BOWL MVP

Finding the right person, whether they're an employee, contractor, or virtual assistant (I'll use the term "team member" for all) is the first major hurdle toward successful delegation. This is one of the most intimidating steps for many business owners, and for good reason—it requires a good amount of time and energy, both of which are probably already scarce. Plus, despite your best attempts, there are no guarantees you'll get it right.

This reality, along with the mental blocks we covered, is why hiring becomes such a bottleneck. The mere thought of posting a job, sifting through dozens or hundreds of applications, and running interviews is enough to make the toughest entrepreneur want to curl up into the fetal position.

What makes this even more challenging is that most business owners wait until they're pulling their hair out before they hire someone. This is the *worst* possible time to hire because desperation kills objectivity. You're prone to rushing the process, lowering your standards, and making emotional decisions, all which increase your chances of making the wrong hire. It's like dating while feeling desperate. You'll settle for someone "good enough" in the moment, even if they're a terrible fit long-term. The result? You hire the wrong person, it's a train wreck, you fire them, and you end up even more burned out and jaded than before.

A smarter approach is to anticipate your hiring needs before they become emergencies. Look ahead and get the process rolling early. Keep an eye out for talent before you need it. Build a bench of quality candidates by keeping a reference file. That way, when the time comes, you're not scrambling.

WHERE TO FIND CANDIDATES

Let's get tactical on where to find qualified candidates. I want you armed with real-life, proven ways to knock this out of the park.

In order of preference, here are my five favorite ways to find quality team members:

1. Personal referrals
2. Clients/customers of your business
3. Other businesses
4. Social media
5. Online job boards

Let's explore each.

PERSONAL REFERRALS

Personal referrals are by far my favorite hiring channel. Many of my best hires came through friends, family, or someone already connected to the organization.

I love referrals because there's a built-in filter. If you have a high-quality friend, they probably have other high-quality friends (birds of a feather). If it's a current team member, they already understand your company's standards, culture, and vision, and so they already know whether the candidate will fit in. Plus, no one close to you is going to recommend someone who could make them look bad.

How do you tap into referrals? Let your network know you're hiring. Ask your current team members, friends, colleagues, and family who they know that could be a fit. Bonus tip: don't stop there. Go one level deeper and ask them to check with *their* inner circle if they know anyone that would be a fit. I've found many great candidates through a "friend of a friend."

CLIENTS/CUSTOMERS OF YOUR BUSINESS

Your best future team members might be paying you right now as customers. Sometimes those who love your business and believe in what you do want to join the team themselves.

Within my company Lifeonaire, our coaches started as members. They already knew our philosophy, values, and processes inside and out. We also got to know them quite well because of the intimate nature of our coaching relationship. Both of these gave us a huge advantage in the hiring process, and in a sense, they'd already been pre-screened. By the same token, members who love what we do have recommended their friends and family to work with us.

As you build strong relationships with your clients and pay attention to who shows passion and alignment with your mission, you might discover that you have a gold mine of potential talent.

OTHER BUSINESSES

I've often found that the best candidates already have jobs. Good people tend to get hired and stay employed. At the same time, don't overlook someone just because they're not working. For all you know, they may have been laid off through no fault of their own, quit because of a toxic boss, or just finished homeschooling their kids. For those that do have jobs, a valuable benefit is that you have the chance to see them in action and observe their performance.

Practically, this means keeping your eyes open for good people as you engage daily with businesses of all types. Quality people reveal themselves everywhere. Notice the waitress who remembers your entire table's orders without writing them down, is on top of drink refills, and does it all while making you feel like a VIP. Or the friendly cashier who smiles and patiently helps a senior citizen with their stack of coupons, despite a growing line of disgruntled customers behind them. Or the contractor who hustles, shows up early, and pays attention to detail. These diamonds are everywhere: the gym, the gas station, the mall, and yes… even the DMV. These are the type of people you want working with you.

If you see the opportunity, you can even "test" them to see how they handle certain situations. For example, overpay with cash at the checkout counter and see if they correct the "mistake" and return the excess. You just learned more about their attention to detail and honesty than a résumé ever could tell you.

When I was actively investing in real estate, I scouted contractors by swinging by the job sites of big homebuilders. If I saw someone who hustled and did quality work, I'd ask if they wanted to make some extra money. I'd go to supply houses and ask the front desk who came in frequently, paid their bills on time, and were easy to work with. They'd give me a list of names. I'd even go to Home Depot at opening to see who was there early, loading up their trucks with materials for the day. You get the idea. The best talent doesn't always walk into your office. You've got to get out there and find it, and it's all around you.

If you use this approach, keep it simple. Compliment their performance and let them know you're always looking for good people. Hand them a business card, and leave the decision in their hands. Most won't call, but some will.

And just to be clear, you're not "poaching." You're simply offering an opportunity. If they're happy, they'll stay where they are. If not, you may have just helped them find a better fit (and found yourself a great team member in the process).

SOCIAL MEDIA

Social media is a powerful hiring tool. A single post announcing an open role can reach hundreds or even thousands of people in your network. Better yet, friends can tag others or share the post, expanding your reach to qualified candidates you'd never otherwise meet.

For a small investment, you can also boost posts and target your audience. Social media may not always deliver the volume of job boards, but the candidates who come in tend to be a bit more pre-qualified because they're closer to your circle. There are also other potential advantages of social media we'll cover when we get to the screening process section.

ONLINE JOB BOARDS

Job boards have their place in finding talent, but based on my experience, they're my least preferred method. Many candidates simply mass-apply without reading the full job description or application instructions, and so you'll likely eliminate 90-plus percent of the applicants right off the bat. That doesn't mean job boards are useless, just set your expectations accordingly.

CHAPTER 21:
HOW TO SCREEN FOR WINNERS

Now that you have your pool of applicants (yay!), you're ready to screen and hire your next Super Bowl–winning teammate.

Again, I know I already said it, but remember that screening and hiring are skills. You probably won't be great when you start, but you'll get better with repetition. And if it's any consolation, most early hires aren't catastrophic if you get it wrong. At this stage, you're probably hiring entry-level roles, so the risk is minimal. If they mess something up or if they don't work out, it won't break the bank or your business. Just think of your first few hires as practice, and it takes the pressure off.

MAKE THEM EARN IT

As a general philosophy, I'm a big fan of making candidates jump through lots of hoops. This approach filters out those who aren't serious and helps ensure you're left with the ones who both qualify *and* really want to be there.

I had a personal experience that strongly illustrated this. Years ago, prior to creating my vision, I wanted to be a full-time firefighter. I was already a part-time volunteer, but I wanted to make it a career. The full-timers warned me that the process was brutal and designed to test your level of commitment. Many of them had failed several times, despite years of previous experience in the fire service. What made this even worse was that there was only one hiring window per year, so if you didn't get selected, you had to wait another full year to apply again.

The process tested both your body and mind. The physical exam alone had 11 challenges including a timed distance run, a 165-pound dummy drag, and a timed four-story staircase ascent while wearing sixty pounds of gear and dragging a hose, just to name a few. Fail any single test, and you were out.

Then came a several-hour written exam where you had to achieve a minimum score of 80 percent to pass. And if you somehow managed to get past both of those, you faced a rapid-fire interview panel with senior leaders.

Oh, and I forgot to mention, this whole process—the tests, the exam, the interview—was spaced out over a period of months. Not days or weeks. *Months.* The success rate from application to getting hired was less than 5 percent. (If you're wondering, I made it all the way to the panel interview but didn't get selected.)

At the time, I thought the process was incredibly inefficient, absurdly extensive, and painfully drawn out. Later, I realized it was brilliant. It was never about just testing skills. It was about testing commitment. The hoops and the delays were there on purpose, and only the people who *truly* wanted it made it through.

Now, I'm not suggesting you design an obstacle course or make people drag dummies across the office. But the principle still stands: high standards protect you and set expectations early. Create a hiring process with multiple steps that challenge applicants enough to reveal who's serious and who's not. Just like a professional sports team doesn't sign a player after one practice, you shouldn't hire after one quick interview call. Make them earn it. The ones who make it through will value the job more, and your chances of landing an A-player go way up.

THE SCREENING TOOLS

Hiring always involves some risk, but you can cut that risk way down by doing your homework upfront with a solid screening process. Yes, this takes effort, but it's far less painful to screen someone out early than fire them later. A little extra work now will save you a ton of time, money, and heartburn down the road.

There is no single, foolproof way to evaluate candidates. That's why I like to use a combination of tools. Think of it as a funnel with a series of filters. You start wide at the top with lots of people, and it gradually narrows more and more until only the best candidates are left.

Here are the screening tools we use and what each one reveals. We'll cover the sequence and timing of the process later. (Note: you don't need to use every tool for every position, so tailor your screening process as needed.)

1. Resume/CV: Basic qualifications and background.
2. Cover letter: Writing ability and motivation.
3. Video submission: Personality, communication, and confidence.
4. Brief interview: Quick filter before investing more time.
5. Work sample: Can they actually do the job?
6. Personality test: Team fit and self-awareness.
7. References: Outside validation of skills, experience, and character.
8. Final interviews: Deep dive into alignment, culture, and long-term potential.

Let's walk through each tool individually, then we'll cover how to combine these into an effective hiring process.

RESUME/CV

We collect resumes, but frankly, I don't place too much stock in them. The reason is they're the professional equivalent of a dating profile. They highlight all the good stuff, but none of the flaws or turn-offs. Applicants share what they want you to know, and very often resumes can exaggerate or dress things up. With a little creativity, you can make almost any task sound impressive. "Mopping the floors" becomes "executed strategic surface transformation initiatives using advanced liquid dispersion techniques."

That doesn't mean resumes are useless; they're just a starting point. When reviewing a resume, look at their job history. Do they jump around a lot? If they're really young, then job-hopping is more common, but if they're past their mid-20s and still bouncing around every few months, that's a red flag that needs a closer look. Turnover is expensive, so you don't want someone who treats your business like a revolving door.

The point is: don't totally ignore resumes, but take them with a grain of salt. They're a good conversation starter, but not a hiring decision-maker.

COVER LETTER

This is where things start to get interesting. A cover letter takes a modest level of effort, so it's a good first swipe at having applicants screen themselves out based on commitment. Many won't follow instructions, so they're removed from the hiring pool.

The best way to use a cover letter is to ask candidates to answer specific questions. This allows you to learn a lot about them early on. For example, consider asking a few of these:

- What do you know about our company, and why do you want this position?
- Why do you think you're the best person for this position?
- Tell us about your current or most recent role. What did you do? What did you like, and what did you not like?
- If you're unemployed, why? If you're employed, why are you looking elsewhere?
- What's the hardest project you've ever worked on? How did it turn out?
- What are the last three books you read?
- What do you do for fun?

These questions reveal motivation, personality, interests, values, and experience. You'd be surprised how much you can learn from a few written answers. If an applicant submits a generic cover letter without answering the questions, they're eliminated.

I'll also include small "hoops" here to test attention to detail. For example, I might ask them to submit both their resume and cover letter in PDF format. Or I'll tell them to write something specific like "your next superstar:)" at the top of their cover letter or in the email subject line. These requests may feel silly to the applicant, but they tell me a lot about how well they follow directions and how much they want the job. Anyone who misses the hoops doesn't move forward in the hiring process.

VIDEO SUBMISSION

I really like video submissions because they show things you'll never see on paper. When you see how someone conducts themselves, you get insights that a resume or cover letter can't provide. And believe me, you'll be amazed at what some people send in.

I once had a woman start her video with, "Ugh, I can't believe I have to make this dumb video." Think she got hired? Not a chance.

Another candidate was applying for a role that required top-notch organizational skills. In his video, I could see stacks of dirty dishes piled up in the sink and cluttered countertops in the background. That said more about his fit for the role than any polished resume ever could.

We typically ask for a 3–5-minute video where they tell us why they want the position, why they feel they're the best fit, and something they're passionate about. Sometimes, we'll even recycle the same questions we used for the cover letter just to see how consistent their answers are. We also request they upload the video as an unlisted link on YouTube and send us that link. If they send it in any other format, they're removed from the pool. Yep, more hoops.

INTERVIEWS

We conduct interviews over video because our team is remote. If you have a local office, I'd suggest doing the interviews in-person, at least in the later rounds.

We use two types of interviews, each at a different stage in the hiring process and each serving a different purpose:

1. Short Interviews (10–15 minutes)

These are quick "nice to meet you" calls early in the hiring process. Their goal isn't to dive deep, but simply to get a general vibe on the person. They're intentionally informal and light, which helps put the candidate at ease. You don't want to misread a good candidate because they're nervous, so the more friendly face time you share, the more chance you'll get to see their real personality.

We share a bit about the company and the role, answer questions, and ask a few easy softball questions about them. These interviews are valuable because if either side discovers it's not a good fit, you'll both save a lot of time and energy by ending things early.

2. Long Interviews (30–45 minutes)

Later in the hiring process, we hold longer, in-depth interviews. This is when we dig in and ask specific questions to scrutinize whether they're the right fit.

We clarify details from their resume, cover letter, or video, and ask targeted questions to uncover their skills, work habits, and motivations. These questions should be challenging enough to expose weaknesses and inconsistencies, but also open enough to let strong candidates shine. By the end of this stage, you should have a clear sense of whether they'd be a valuable, long-term addition to your team.

For a list of real-life interview questions we use in our interviews, go to BusinessForLife.com.

WORK SAMPLE

Resumes and interviews only go so far. To really assess someone's skills, we'll ask for examples of past work and a small work sample. For many roles, it's fair and very useful to ask candidates to do a simple task that mirrors the job.

- Graphic designer? Ask them to create a social media image.
- Video editor? Edit a short raw clip.
- Sales manager? Have them review a few sales calls and point out areas for improvement.

You can give them a window (12–24 hours) to complete the task, or, even better, have them do it live while you watch. I prefer live because it doesn't just reveal skills and speed, but also how they think and handle pressure.

As a rule of thumb, keep work samples small—something that should take 15–20 minutes. Don't use them for free labor. If you want a larger or more complex task, that's fine, but pay them for it.

PERSONALITY TEST

Personality assessments aren't required, but they can add helpful insight. Tools like DISC, Myers-Briggs, Enneagram, StrengthsFinder, Predictive Index, and Kolbe are widely used. These help paint a picture of how a candidate may think, work, and relate to others.

We'll typically just choose one assessment to avoid complicating the process. The goal isn't to put someone in a box or automatically reject them, but to see how well their natural style matches the job.

For example, on the DISC test, a "High I" is usually outgoing, people-oriented, and persuasive, but not super organized or detail-oriented.

That might be fantastic for a customer-facing position, but not ideal for a quiet, heads-down job that requires attention to detail.

Personality tests shouldn't be the deciding factor in your hiring decision, but they could be a valuable tie-breaker when you're weighing candidates with similar qualifications.

REFERENCES

Checking references is important, but there are two major drawbacks to keep in mind. First, your applicant hand-picked them, so there's a really good chance they've only selected people who will say good things. And second, professional references may be reluctant (or even prohibited) to say anything negative due to fear of legal ramifications.

That doesn't mean you should skip them. Just realize they may be biased or vague, so you'll have to "pull the thread" by asking follow-up questions. You don't have to perform a CIA-level interrogation, but don't settle for surface answers either. Listen to *how* they answer as much as *what* they say. Do they hesitate? What are they *not* saying? By tuning in and approaching the discussion with genuine curiosity, you'll get answers you can use.

We like to get a balanced perspective by collecting three types of references: (1) family, (2) friends, and (3) professional contacts.

This allows us to cross-reference statements and look for consistency. If someone's personal and professional lives tell very different stories, that's a red flag. If John works at the church but he spends every night getting hammered at the casinos, that would spark concern and warrant a closer look.

On the professional side, we want to speak with their boss, peers, and direct reports (if applicable). We want to see a 360-degree view of how they lead, follow, and function as part of a team.

Here are a few example questions to get you started:

- If you had to describe [candidate] in three to five words, what would they be?
- In your opinion, what are the candidate's strengths? Where have you seen those strengths in action?
- Where do you think they might struggle, and why?
- Did they fit the culture of your workplace? How so?
- If they applied at your business again, knowing what you know now, would you have made the same hiring decision?

BACKGROUND CHECKS

As a final step, we conduct both credit and criminal background checks. Some business owners may hesitate here, especially with credit checks, because they worry it feels invasive. But here's the reality: if someone is going to handle your company's money or be in a position that requires financial trust, you need confidence in their reliability and judgment. You're not looking for an 800-credit score. Life happens. People lose jobs, get sick, and have unexpected expenses. What you're looking for are patterns that raise questions about responsibility and stability. And if something concerning pops up, just talk about it. A simple, open conversation may clear everything up.

We once had a great applicant who passed the screening process with flying colors, until we got to the credit check. We found a recent string of late payments and a low credit score. Normally, that might have been alarming, but because the candidate had been upfront with us about the situation in advance and explained the reasons behind it, it wasn't a dealbreaker. We hired them anyway, and they turned out to be fantastic.

Similarly, you may encounter a candidate with legal trouble in the past or even time in prison. That doesn't mean you have to automatically disqualify them. Ask for the story, listen, and make an informed, context-influenced decision.

Use background checks to protect your business and provide insight, but weigh the results alongside other factors. Lastly, remember you must always get written permission and comply with local laws before conducting any kind of background check.

THE SCREENING PROCESS

Now that you're familiar with the tools for screening applicants, let's look at how to combine them into a clear, step-by-step, effective hiring process.

At every stage, your goal is simple: eliminate anyone who doesn't pass with flying colors. Only the strongest candidates are allowed to move forward. If you reach the end of your process and no one is a clear-cut, enthusiastic "yes," then the answer is "no." Don't hire anyone. Don't try to convince yourself they're "good enough." You're not looking for average. You're looking for an A-player.

Also, never hire someone because they're the best of the current batch. Hiring the top pick from a weak applicant pool is like only choosing a spouse from your neighborhood. If you don't find the right person, go back to the drawing board and start again. Refine your job description, try different channels, or simply repost later. Sometimes it's just a timing issue, and relisting a couple of weeks later brings in a completely different pool. One extra month of searching for the right hire is better than wasting months onboarding and training the wrong one. You'll just end up firing them and starting all over anyway. Doing it on the front end saves you time, money, frustration, and unnecessarily hurt feelings.

One last thing: regardless of the outcome (whether they move forward or are eliminated), be sure to communicate quickly, clearly, and kindly. This keeps your hiring experience professional, transparent, and respectful. Just because someone isn't a fit now doesn't mean they won't be a great fit in the future for a different role, so treat everyone well.

Step 1: Resume, Cover Letter, and Short Video Submission

You'll likely lose 70-plus percent of your applicants here because they'll either not follow instructions correctly, or they'll skip a part. That's fine. Those who submit everything successfully and show promise advance to the next step. At this stage we're looking for completeness, effort, professionalism, and basic alignment with the role.

Importantly, although this might be obvious, always screen every candidate using the exact same criteria. Give everyone a fair shot and the same opportunity. Anything less is unfair, bad business, and can get you in hot water legally.

Step 2: Short Virtual Interview and Online Presence Review

Candidates who pass the first stage are invited to a short, informal video chat (10–15 minutes). This is usually conducted by a team member, not the final decision-maker. The purpose is simply to get acquainted, talk lightly about the role, ask a few questions, and answer theirs. It should feel conversational, not high-stakes. During this call, it's wise to touch on compensation to make sure it's a fit.

For those who show promise, we'll also do a brief, public online search afterward. We're not doing a Magnum P.I.-level investigation; we're just checking for obvious red flags. If nothing alarming is discovered, they advance to the next step.

Step 3: Work Sample

Depending on the role, we ask candidates to submit a work sample. This can be previous representative work, and/or a small task that mirrors the job's responsibilities. If it's a task, either have them complete it within a short window of time, or just do it live with you on the line watching. Always assign the same task to every applicant so you're comparing apples to apples.

Step 4: Personality Assessment

Whether it's DISC, Kolbe, Myers-Briggs, or another tool, have the candidate complete a personality assessment. There's usually a small fee, but it's worth the small investment. Again, these aren't pass/fail. They are just another lens that helps you see how someone naturally operates and aligns with the role's demands.

Step 5: Reference Checks

At this point, you'll probably be down to only a handful of strong candidates. Now we check references. We typically like to speak with three to five people, spanning friends, family, and professional connections. The goal here is to gather a balanced, multi-angle perspective of the candidate and look for consistency in how people describe them.

Step 6: Final Interviews

Candidates who reach this stage go through two to three interviews with a mix of current team members. We intentionally select both those who will work closely with the new hire, as well as those who won't. This blend provides a more well-rounded, objective assessment. The final interview is conducted with the senior leader of the department.

Afterward, all interviewers collaboratively discuss the applicant to make a hiring decision. If even one person raises serious concerns, we slow down, investigate further, or pass.

During final interviews, be picky. You're not just looking for someone who can do the job, you want someone who can crush the job. You should feel like you *need* this person on your team and wonder, *Where have you been all my life*?

Step 7: Background Checks

If your candidate makes it this far, they're one step away from the offer. You like them, feel confident in their abilities and fit, and if they pass the criminal and credit background checks, you've found your next team member. Congratulations!

FINAL HIRING TIPS

Here are a few last-minute tips and reminders to boost your chances of making a good hire:

- **Don't hire out of emotion.** Stay objective. Just because you and a candidate both have a wiener dog, doesn't mean they're the right fit. And if you're desperate, exhausted, or overwhelmed with work, be extra careful. Resist the urge to hire the first person who raises their hand.

- **Take your time.** Rushing the process almost always backfires. Saying "no" early is far less painful for everyone than having to let them go later.
- **Don't hire someone who can't afford to work with you.** If they need more income than you can afford to pay, they'll eventually leave, no matter how much they love your company and mission. This is a real concern, especially if your company has a great reputation and people want to work with you. Don't let excitement blind either of you to financial reality.
- **Don't hire a clone of yourself.** It's natural to gravitate toward people who think and act like you, but hiring another version of you just duplicates blind spots and overlap. There's also a good chance they're not going to like the very tasks you're trying to hand off. Instead, look for someone whose skills and strengths complement your own.
- **Don't ignore small red flags.** Little red flags can signal big problems down the road. If someone shows up casually late, complains excessively about their former boss, doesn't ask any thoughtful questions, or seems evasive, listen to your Spidey-senses. Something is off.
- **Prioritize flexibility.** In a small, growing business, roles and responsibilities shift. You don't want someone with a "that's not my job" mentality. Look for people who are willing to roll up their sleeves, pitch in, and grow as the company grows.
- **Use a 90-day probation period.** Make it clear up front that the first three months are a "no harm no foul" trial period for both sides. This gives the new hire permission to bow out

without feeling bad if the role isn't what they expected, and it allows you to assess whether they're meeting your expectations without guilt.

In closing, remember that hiring isn't just about filling a seat. It's about intentionally building a team that will allow you to create a business you love. The right people multiply your impact, protect your time, and strengthen your culture. The wrong ones drain your energy, slow you down, and make you want to pull your hair out. So be patient, be picky, stay objective, and choose wisely.

CHAPTER 22:
ONBOARDING YOUR NEW ROCKSTAR

iring the right people is a huge win, but we're not done yet. Now it's time to bring them onto the field and into the game with solid onboarding. This stage sets the right tone for your entire working relationship. Even the best of hires can start to doubt their decision if their first few weeks are confusing, disorganized, or discouraging, so give this your full attention.

Let's begin by being very clear: onboarding isn't just about paperwork, handing them a stack of standard operating procedures (SOPs), or giving an office tour. It's about setting up your new hire for success, connecting them to your mission, and building momentum quickly. Do yourself (and your new hire) a huge favor and have an onboarding process set up in advance. You do not want to wing this.

An onboarding process should include four major pillars:

1. A warm welcome
2. Orientation to the company
3. Role clarity and expectations
4. Role-specific training

A WARM WELCOME

Think back to your first day of high school: new place, new people, and zero clue where you belong. You don't want your new hire feeling like that. Go above and beyond to make them feel welcomed, valued, and that they're in the right place.

Introduce them to the team and set the tone. Share with the team why you're excited about bringing them onboard. Have each team member share their name, role, a bit about themselves, and a fun fact to break the ice. Also encourage your team members to follow up later and get to know the new hire as a person, not just as part of the company. Since your team was already involved in making the hiring decision, this shouldn't be difficult.

Remember: people don't stay at their jobs for a paycheck unless they're forced to. They stay for the relationships. You want your new hire to love working with you.

ORIENTATION TO THE COMPANY

Even if you've shared your mission, purpose, and values during the hiring process, go over these again with the new hire. Reignite their passion and reinforce their decision to join your team. Talk about your culture and make them excited to be part of something special.

In addition:

- Give them an overview of all the moving parts of the business. Consider showing them your BAM so they understand how everything fits together.

- Complete the HR stuff (employment/independent contractor agreement, code of conduct, payroll, etc.)

ROLE CLARITY AND EXPECTATIONS

From day one, they need to know exactly what "winning" looks like. They need to be crystal clear on expectations, how they'll be evaluated, and how they'll be held accountable. There's no room for ambiguity or tiptoeing around here.

Cover:

- **Key responsibilities.** A prioritized list of their daily/weekly/monthly activities, as well as large quarterly projects that they'll be part of.
- **Mission tie-in.** Clarify how their role supports the bigger picture and emphasize why they're important to the company's success.
- **Boundaries and authority.** What decisions and actions they can make on their own, and what needs approval. This prevents micromanagement and costly mistakes.
- **Communication expectations.** Indicate the preferred method(s) of communication (email, group chat, etc.) and the preferred chain of communication (who they should go to with questions or problems).

I cannot stress this enough: they need to know *exactly* what's expected of them and the required output of their position. Be kind but clear as you communicate this.

After you've gone through everything, have them repeat back what they heard. I'd recommend you have everything in writing as well. If they don't fully understand how to rock out this role, I guarantee you both will end up frustrated and have a negative experience.

ROLE-SPECIFIC TRAINING

Practically speaking, training is usually pretty straightforward. Most of it boils down to a simple, hands-on process where independence is gained as trust and competence are proven. Kinda anticlimactic, I know, but it doesn't have to be any more complicated than that.

Let's break training into three easy-to-remember steps—the 3 "Ss" of training:

Step 1. Shadow

Your new hire begins by observing you (or the current role holder) perform the task. Don't just show them *what* to do, but take the time to explain *why* you're doing it. Point out common mistakes and where they might slip up. Help them understand the logic behind the task and how it contributes to the bigger picture. People are far more motivated when they know their work matters, so the more you can convey the importance of a task, the more invested they'll be in doing it well.

Encourage note-taking during this process, and have them follow along with the SOP if one exists (more on that later). If you don't have one yet, consider recording yourself performing the task and have your new hire draft the SOP as part of their learning.

Step 2. Supervised

Now it's their turn. They perform the task under your supervision, referring to their notes and the SOP for guidance. You're there to answer questions as needed, but ideally, they can complete it with minimal (or no) input from you. Many people learn best by doing, so this is where they'll work out kinks and gain confidence in their ability.

During this time, if they make a mistake, it's important to correct them immediately. Don't wait until a multi-step task is fully completed and then give them a list of 12 things they messed up. Instead, give them one piece of feedback at a time, have them re-do it correctly, then move forward. Repeat this until the entire process is completed successfully. This builds confidence and competence much more quickly.

Step 3. Solo

At this point, they've shown they can perform the task correctly and you both feel they're ready to fly solo. Give them full ownership and let them run with it. Be available if they need help, but unless problems arise, there's no further need to check in.

Here's where it can get even better: if you've hired the right person and built the right culture, they won't just execute the task, they'll improve it. They may discover faster, smarter, or easier ways of doing things. When this happens, recognize and reward their initiative. Update the SOP and give them credit (publicly if possible) for the improvement.

Remember that for this to happen, you must be open to new approaches and resist the "this is how it's always been done" mentality. Many times, breakthroughs and growth come from fresh thinking—not rigidly clinging to old approaches.

Let me also address one last thing: micromanagement. Don't do it. No one likes a boss hovering over their shoulder and nitpicking every move. It's belittling and reflects more on you than them. If you don't trust them to do the job correctly, either there's a problem with your hiring, onboarding, or training process, or you're holding on to trauma from previous hires and taking it out on them.

CHAPTER 23:
CREATE YOUR SOP PLAYBOOK

et's go back to my friend Joe with the rental portfolio in Birmingham. After telling me he'd designed his business to serve his life, I was eager to hear how.

"The first thing I did was figure out how much money I'd need to live my vision," Joe said. "Then I worked out how many rentals I'd need to hit that number."

Simple enough, I thought. "Got it. And what do you personally do in the business? What does a typical day look like?" I asked.

He grinned. "Well, I can tell you what I *don't* do… I don't do renovation estimates. I don't deal with subcontractors. I don't handle applications, showings, or leases. I don't talk to tenants, and I definitely don't do repairs or maintenance."

"Uh… so what *do* you do?" I asked, unsure what was left to running the business.

Joe chuckled, "Well…get paid, I guess."

We both laughed, but I wasn't satisfied. "Seriously, how are you able to be so hands-off? Most people would love to be in your shoes, but they're chained to their business 24–7. What's your secret?"

He didn't hesitate. "Delegation and checklists."

"Delegation and checklists?" I repeated, a little disappointed. It sounded too easy.

"Yup. That's it."

He saw my confusion, so he explained. "See, when I was in the military, everything ran off checklists. They had teenagers running nuclear submarines worth hundreds of millions of dollars. I was one of them. None of us had a clue, and the military knew it. That's why they relied so heavily on systems and documentation."

He went on: "We were trained, and then expected to follow the protocol. Even if you'd done a task a thousand times, you *still* were required to have the manual in front of you. If you were caught without it, you were immediately fired, even if you did the task perfectly. That discipline made sure things were done right—every time. I just brought that same system into my business."

It started to click.

"Walk me through how you did this." I asked.

"When I first started the business, I didn't know how to do anything. So I forced myself to learn it all. Once I had the basics down, I focused on doing each task the same way every single time. I tweaked, refined, and systemized until the process was predictable. Then, I created simple step-by-step checklists for every task. No one is going to read a 20-page manual, but everyone can follow a short checklist."

He continued: "Once the checklists were done, I started hiring. Every time I handed off a task, I had confidence it would be done right since the system was already proven. And with each new delegation, I'd ask myself *"Of the tasks still left on my plate, how can I never need to do this again?"* And over time, I freed myself from the business and grew it to where it is today."

Suddenly it all seemed so simple…and genius. Delegation requires clear tasks, and the simplest way to create that clarity is with short, checklist-style SOPs. They're quick to create, easy for your team to follow, and the most foolproof way to make sure nothing slips between the cracks.

Think of SOP as standing for "Same Outcome, Predictably." When created and used properly, they improve clarity and organization, while also reducing confusion and mistakes. Well-designed SOPs are also one of the biggest reasons why franchises have a higher success rate than mom and pop businesses. They operate on proven systems, not memory, talent, or guesswork.

Now, I know the word "SOP" doesn't exactly inspire excitement. For many, it feels boring, corporate, or a waste of time. But here's the truth: SOP is just a business word for *recipe*. In this case though, instead of baking a cake, you're building something way yummier—a business that can run without you. And just like your favorite cookbook is a collection of all your best recipes, your business needs its own vault of SOPs that provide step-by-step instructions for your team.

CREATE YOUR SOPS WITH THE FOUR CS

In a perfect world, your SOPs would have already been created before you bring someone onboard. But if not, no worries. Creating these can be one of the first tasks your new hire helps with. Just follow the simple "Four Cs" process:

Step 1: Capture

Do the task yourself, and while you're doing it, record the process. Use screen-recording, video, or audio (whatever is most suitable). As you perform the task, talk through it.

Explain:

- What you're doing
- Why it's important
- Why you do it that way
- What mistakes to look out for

Recording is far better than writing from memory, which almost always leaves out details. Another option is to have someone look over your shoulder and write down each step while asking clarifying questions.

Side note: Except in rare cases, I'm not a big fan of having SOPs in video format. Videos are slow to reference when someone just needs one quick detail, and hard to update when things change. If you want to include video snippets, make them short and include them as part of a text-based SOP. This way, your team benefits from both the ease and clarity of a checklist, as well as a visual example when valuable.

Step 2: Convert

Once you've captured the recording, it's time to convert it into something usable. There's no need to do this manually since AI tools can handle this instantly and far more accurately. Take the transcript then drop it into a document format. I prefer cloud-based SOPs because this way everyone is sure to be working from the same, most up-to-date version.

Step 3: Clean Up

Next, take the transcript and refine it to be user-friendly and practical. Think clarity and simplicity. Break it down into numbered steps and bullet points. Use bold text to highlight critical actions, drop in links, or add brief commentary if they'll help.

One of the biggest questions I get is: *"How much detail should I include?"* The answer is just enough for someone to complete the task correctly, and nothing more. Lean, concise, and practical beat bloated every time. A great test is to ask a 15-year-old to follow it and see if they can do the task as directed. If they can, you're good to go. If not, find the gaps or confusing sections and fix them.

Step 4: Catalog

You're done! Now just file it in a shared online folder everyone can access. Inside that master "SOP" folder, create subfolders for the major areas of the business. For example: customer service, marketing, web/tech, finance, and so on.

If you want to be a ninja, hyperlink your BAM (Business Architecture Map) action items to their matching SOPs. This ties your big-picture strategy to the tactical steps that make it happen.

This four-step process is simple, straightforward, and it works. Don't overcomplicate it. I've seen way too many well-meaning entrepreneurs write out crazy 20-page SOPs that do nothing but collect digital dust. (Which is a double whammy because nobody uses them *and* you wasted a whole lot of time, money, and effort creating them.)

Reinforce a culture of using SOPs every day; not because you don't trust them, but because it's an easy way to reduce avoidable mistakes while saving brainpower for other things. Even if someone has done a task a hundred times, they should be following the SOP. Someone makes a mistake? The first question you ask should be: "Did you follow the SOP?" If they answer "yes", then update it because something needs to be fixed. If "no", coach them back to using it. This creates accountability while ensuring your SOPs stay current.

And lastly, remember that not everything needs an SOP. One-off or rare tasks aren't usually worth the effort. Instead, only document the core parts of the business that are done often and serve a valuable function.

Ok, now that you understand the onboarding process, training, and SOPs, let's go through a few last tips for successful delegation, then wrap it up with how to handle things when they go wrong.

CHAPTER 24: DELEGATION MASTERY

Congratulations. You now have a complete A-to-Z framework for effective delegation. Before we wrap up though, here are a few final insights to help you build your team of rockstars.

START SMALL AND SAFE

If you're new to delegation, you're probably not going to nail it right out of the gate. You'll make mistakes; sometimes in who you hire, sometimes in what you delegate, and sometimes in how you communicate. It's a normal part of the process.

Your goal in the beginning is simple: keep your "mistake tax" low while you learn. Practically speaking, the best way to do that is start with small, simple, and safe. Hire for low-risk, low-skill, low-cost positions first. These early hires allow you to practice delegation without putting the business at major risk.

This approach gives you three big advantages:

1. Low risk: If something goes wrong, it won't significantly harm the business.
2. Low skill requirement: It's much easier to find and train someone for these roles.

3. Low cost: These hires are less expensive. You'll gain experience in the process and free up your time without breaking the bank.

Think of these early hires as your delegation "training wheels." They free you from low-value work while also giving you a safe runway to hone your delegation skills.

SET THE CULTURE EARLY AND OFTEN

Culture isn't something that develops by accident. You build it intentionally and protect it fiercely. Decide what you want your company to stand for and what's important, and bake it into the company's DNA.

If you want a culture of excellence, trust, teamwork, ownership, and growth, it's on you to create that through repetition and consistency. Model those traits, and reinforce them through praise, recognition, and accountability.

Equally important is addressing toxic behaviors immediately. Don't ignore them or assume they'll fade with time, because they won't. They'll spread like a cancer in your organization. I've led teams where distrust, entitlement, and apathy took root. I buried my head in the sand, hoping I could avoid confrontation, but it just got worse. It wasn't until I stepped in and had some hard conversations that things improved.

Create an environment where your team feels valued, challenged, and supported; something they're excited to be part of. Celebrate wins together and give recognition for a job well done. Encourage open sharing and dialogue. Check in with them regularly, and develop a personal relationship beyond the workplace. The closer you are as a team and the more you genuinely care for each other, the more fun you'll have and the better everyone will show up.

PRIORITIZE COMMUNICATION

Open, respectful, honest, and frequent communication is critical to the success of every business. Without it, misunderstandings pile up, tension builds, and morale and performance drop.

Your team must feel safe sharing feedback, ideas, concerns, and mistakes without fear of judgment or repercussions. Otherwise, you're inviting gossip, frustration and disengagement into your organization. You want people to bring issues to the surface, not whisper about them in the background or keep them to themselves.

To prevent this, you need to model transparency and approachability. Genuinely encourage your team to share, and be receptive when people speak up. Listen carefully and fully before responding, and acknowledge their input, even if you don't agree with it. If you react harshly or shut people down, they won't speak up again and you'll lose out on their future contributions.

I vividly remember a mistake I made early on in this area that changed how I communicate to this day. I had recently transitioned from being a coach in Lifeonaire to CEO. One day, during a call with the coaching team, I abruptly shut down a new coach's idea. I didn't think much of it at the time. I was just trying to move the meeting along.

But after the call ended, a senior coach I respected pulled me aside. He reminded me that I wasn't just "one of the coaches" anymore— I was CEO. And that meant my words and actions carried far more weight and impact than when I was a peer.

That conversation hit me hard. I realized that as a leader, *everything* we say or do matters. And because of that, we have the power to either build up or break down our team, culture, and business with the way we communicate.

ENCOURAGE INDEPENDENT THOUGHT AND ACTION

One of the single most valuable things you can do as a leader is to help your team learn how to think, make decisions, and act on their own. Without that, you'll always be the bottleneck, no matter how many people you hire. You don't want a team of mindless minions. That's what automation is for. You want problem-solvers—people who spot issues, propose solutions, and take initiative without needing you to hold their hand. These folks are worth their weight in gold and will transform your business.

As you embrace this, realize you're not just training problem-solving and independence. You're building a sense of ownership. When you hand over both the task *and* the responsibility for the outcome, people become more invested. They feel trusted and take a sense of pride in their work. They become move vested in their role and the success of the company.

The way you build this behavior is by mentorship and encouragement. Openly share your decision-making process with your team. Explain your rationale when approaching a situation. Let them see *how* you think, not just *what* you decided.

Put this into practice as soon as possible. Start by giving them small, low-risk decisions, and as their confidence and competence grows, give them bigger decisions and more responsibility.

As a practical way to foster independent thinking, whenever a team member brings you a problem, don't just give them the answer. Instead, ask: "What do *you* think you should do?" and see what they come up with. Push the thinking back to them. If you do this consistently, they'll start coming to you only after they've already thought through a few options. If their idea is solid, go with it. If not, help them see what they missed or how to improve their reasoning. Over time, they'll come to you less and less, and eventually not at all, which is the goal.

Before long, your team won't just solve problems, they'll spot issues before they even become problems. They'll notice areas to eliminate, automate, or delegate. They'll start seeing things you missed. At some point, maybe they'll even respectfully challenge your thinking and offer something even better. That, my friend, is a great day.

Don't sabotage this. Don't let your own insecurities, need to be right, or desire for control keep your team on a leash. You must learn to let go and resist the urge to meddle or micromanage. Yes, people will make mistakes (more on that in the next section), but you can't just swoop back in the moment someone messes up. Imagine if the first time your toddler fell over when learning how to walk you just decided, "Nah... this isn't for you kid." Same goes here.

CHAPTER 25:
WHEN THINGS DON'T GO AS PLANNED

L et's get this out of the way: your team will mess up. They'll miss details, drop the ball, and misunderstand instructions. They'll do things that you didn't want them to, and not do the things you did. Not because they're bad, but because they're human, just like you and me. When (not *if*) this happens, how you respond will shape both your company culture and future success.

MISTAKES ARE GOLD MINES

Although many business owners prefer that mistakes never happen, I see them differently. Mistakes are gold mines. They're an opportunity to learn, improve, and strengthen your systems. They reveal cracks in the business and shine a spotlight on areas that need attention.

Although it can feel frustrating when a mistake is made, I encourage you to look at the silver lining and even get excited because it's like getting free business consulting, telling you exactly what to fix. And every time you diagnose the cause and make the improvement, the odds of it happening again go down. Over time, your business graduates from making the same mistakes to making new ones, and the business moves forward.

Addressing mistakes can be uncomfortable, especially if you tend to avoid conflict. But you're doing your team and business a huge disservice by avoiding these conversations. Each and every mistake, no matter how big or small, should be analyzed for its cause. Otherwise, not only will it happen again, but perhaps even worse, you're creating a culture where accountability, excellence, and constant improvement aren't valued. It's not fair to your team either. They want to do well and get better, but they can't do that if they don't get feedback.

One more benefit of this "no mistake left behind" philosophy is that your team will start holding themselves to a higher standard. They'll take more ownership over their work, examine their own performance, identify mistakes, and proactively look for areas for improvement. I love hearing about fixed mistakes that I didn't even know about.

To be successful with this approach, it's important that you remove emotion from the situation. When you discover a mistake or one is brought to your attention, let go of any frustration, disappointment, or judgment. These will prevent you from assessing the situation objectively and often lead to reactions you'll regret. Even if this error has happened more than once and you feel there's no good reason for it, blowing up doesn't solve anything. Blaming, degrading, or pointing fingers only damages relationships and morale.

Instead, a more effective approach is to imagine you're a detective investigating a crime scene. Carefully and tactfully retrace the steps that led to the mistake, in as non-accusatory a manner as possible. Stay calm, curious, and factual. Ask simple, neutral questions:

- "Did you follow the SOP?"
- "What led to this?"
- "Walk me through what happened."

Remember, you're not looking for someone to blame—you're looking for the behavior or structural reason for the mistake.

This leads to another important tip: take responsibility first. Before you assume it's your team's fault, look for your contribution to the mistake.

Ask yourself:

- *Was I clear on what I wanted and why it mattered?*
- *Have I provided the right training, tools, and support?*
- *Is the SOP clear and up to date?*
- *Did I communicate priorities and deadlines?*
- *Did something outside their control hold them up?*
- *Do they have too much on their plate?*
- *Have I created a safe space for questions?*

Notice most of these questions are about you, not them. And at least from my experience, you'll be surprised at how often the trail leads back to the person in the mirror. That realization may sting, but it's also incredibly empowering because if you're part of the problem, you can create the solution.

I learned this approach by doing the opposite. I used to blame others and think: "They didn't listen!" or "They messed up!" But all that did was frustrate me and weaken the culture of my team. It wasn't until I stepped back and looked for my part first that everything changed. Maybe *I* didn't set expectations clearly enough. Maybe *I* didn't explain the process well. Maybe *I* didn't set them up for success.

The approach I use now is when I see my contribution, I take ownership and apologize to my team. I also find ways to avoid making the same mistake again. Incredibly, this has caused my team to do the same. Instead of pointing fingers, they now look to find their part in the problem. This allows all of us to grow together and create a culture of accountability and responsibility.

WHY DELEGATION BREAKS DOWN

Now that we've covered how to handle mistakes, let's look at the most common causes. Assuming you've hired the right person, most delegation issues can be tracked back to one of four root sources:

1. Information
2. Communication
3. Organization
4. Motivation

Lucky for us, these are usually easy to spot. And once you fix one, the benefits ripple across the entire company, since the same issue tends to show up in more than one place.

Information

When mistakes stem from information issues, the person simply doesn't know *how* to complete the task. They have the ability, just not the knowledge. These issues usually stem from poor training and/or documentation. To fix this,

- Make sure to use the three "Ss" delegation process outlined earlier (Shadow, Supervised, Solo).
- Have clear, up-to-date, user-friendly SOPs.
- Encourage your team members to reference the SOP while performing the task.

Just like orchestra musicians keep sheet music in front of them even if they've memorized the part, your team should use SOPs as they work. This improves consistency and reveals where instructions are still unclear.

It's important to note that sometimes what looks like an information problem is really a culture problem. In these cases, team members don't feel comfortable saying "I don't understand this." They worry about disappointing you, looking bad, or getting reprimanded. This is a leadership issue, and it falls on you. Have you made it safe to ask questions? Do you respond patiently when someone admits they're confused? If people are scared to speak up, they'll guess, which leads to mistakes. Normalize asking questions and open dialog. Reward honesty and candor. Otherwise, you'll never know what's really going on in your business or with your team members.

Communication

Sometimes the issue isn't know-how; it's the lack of systems and guardrails to support execution. In these cases, people struggle to complete tasks because they're distracted, disorganized, or overwhelmed.

Here are some practical tips to fix organizational issues:

- Build out a clear task list for each team member

  - Add information including:
    - Daily, weekly, monthly, and quarterly responsibilities
    - Priority level (low, medium, high)
    - Due date and expected time to complete
    - Progress status (not started, in progress, complete)
    - Collaborators and resources required

- Make sure their work environment supports productivity. Is it quiet, clean, and organized? Or noisy, cluttered, and full of distractions?

- Have a well-organized folder and file and naming convention for all documentation that is easily searchable.
- Avoid overwhelming your team with competing priorities. Confusion about what matters most originates from you.

Lastly, don't overlook the human factor. Some people simply struggle with focus more than others. Coaching and mentoring around time management, focus techniques, and better use of tools can assist here.

Organization

Communication issues are both very common and very easy to prevent. Most often, they result from a misunderstanding around *what* needed to be done, *how* it should be done, or *when* you wanted it done.

Challenges with communication are solved by clear, concise, documented communication. Every time you assign a task, be sure to clarify the deadline, its priority in relation to everything else, and the exact output you expect. Then, confirm understanding by having your team member repeat back what they heard and write it down. This is one of the simplest and easiest ways to avoid confusion.

Finally, it bears repeating: make it safe to ask questions. Asking early is always better than fixing later.

Motivation

The final common cause of mistakes is motivation—when someone *can* do the task, but doesn't *want* to. This one is trickier because it's rooted in emotion rather than a lack of skill, systems, or dialogue, but it's still solvable.

Some typical reasons include:

- They feel the task is boring or "beneath" them.
- They dislike the task because it doesn't come naturally to them.
- They don't see the value in completing it.
- They're distracted by personal issues.

Your job as a leader is to dig beneath the surface and uncover why they're unmotivated. Don't assume laziness, stubbornness, or intentional disrespect. Instead, approach with genuine curiosity and a calm, non-confrontational tone. You're more likely to discover the root issue when the person feels they can be open and honest with you.

THE CRUX OF ADDRESSING ISSUES

When addressing problems, always remember this: your team members are people, not machines. They're someone's daughter, son, spouse, or parent. They have lives outside of work and experience loss, conflict, exhaustion, and anxiety, just like you. That's why every situation should be handled with grace, empathy, and patience. A good rule of thumb is to treat your team the way you'd want your own child's boss to treat them. Meet people where they are, come alongside them, and work together to help fix the problem.

At the same time, this doesn't mean lowering the bar. You must balance compassion with performance, grace with accountability, and empathy with excellence. It's a constant balance act that requires practice, intention, and continual adjustment.

Hey, no one said leadership was easy, right? But that's what makes great leaders rare and valuable.

FIRING TEAM MEMBERS

I'm not going to sugarcoat it; firing someone is one of the most emotionally difficult parts of leadership (at least it is for me). These are real people with real lives. They have families, mortgages, and medical bills. Knowing that your decision affects not just them, but the people who depend on them, can feel gut-wrenching.

And yet, if you want to protect your business, your team, and your customers, you can't avoid it. Letting go of people is part of your job description, and no matter how well you hire, train, and lead, if you work with people long enough, it's inevitable.

The best advice I can give you is this: once you've given someone a fair chance to improve and they still haven't stepped up, it's time to let them go. I've stumbled here more times than I care to admit. Despite clear signs they weren't the right person, I'd keep giving extra chances, hoping they'd turn things around. And by the time I finally took action, I'd wasted months of time and energy that could've been spent supporting the rest of my team and growing the business.

I once asked a seasoned C-suite executive how he handled firing, and he said *"I've never fired anyone. I've just delivered the news."* That perspective has helped me quite a bit with handling letting people go. I used to struggle with feeling like the bad guy, but this reframes the situation as being their choice, not yours. If you've clearly communicated expectations, provided reasonable support and training, and still see no meaningful progress, it's time to either move them into a role that's better fit for their strengths or part ways.

Keeping someone who isn't performing doesn't just hurt your profitability, it damages your culture. When others see poor performance tolerated, it sends the message that excellence and accountability don't really matter, and over time that erodes trust, morale, and your credibility as a leader. In this way, firing isn't about cruelty; it's about stewardship. It's about protecting the health of the business, honoring the effort of those who *are* performing, and making sure that every seat on your team is filled by someone who truly belongs there.

TOP FIVE DELEGATION MISTAKES TO AVOID

We already know that delegation is more challenging than elimination and automation, so it's no surprise that there are plenty of ways it can go sideways. Don't let that scare you though. Once you experience the freedom, leverage, and growth that come from effective delegation, you'll never want to go back to doing everything yourself.

As we wrap up, here's an overview of the five big delegation mistakes to watch out for:

Delegation Mistake #1: Not Delegating at All

By far, the number one mistake is clinging to the "I'll just do it myself" mentality. This approach is short-sighted and guarantees you'll always have a job, but never a business. It also guarantees you'll hit an early ceiling and your business will fall short of what it's capable of. Even if delegation feels uncomfortable at first, bring someone onboard and start small. Delegate low-risk, low-impact tasks and build your confidence from there. Yes, you'll make mistakes. But the alternative is far worse:

staying stuck as a one-person show and never experiencing the freedom that entrepreneurship is supposed to provide.

Delegation Mistake #2: Delegating Too Late

Finding, screening, hiring, onboarding, and training the right people takes time, so don't wait until you're desperate. Start looking for someone early, before you're overwhelmed (or even better, before you need someone). If you needed help yesterday, you've waited too long and your chances of making an emotional decision skyrocket.

Also, it's worth saying this again: If you don't have a clear "yes," at the end of the process, don't hire anyone. Choosing the best person from a weak pool is still a bad hire. Instead, refine your approach and start the process over again. It's frustrating in the moment, but far less painful than hiring the wrong person.

Delegation Mistake #3: Abdicating Instead of Delegating

Delegation isn't dumping a pile of tasks on someone then walking away. That's abdication, and it won't give you the results you're hoping for.

I've seen it happen time after time: a new team member is brought on without any real plan, and it's a disaster from the very start. They're not onboarded or trained well, they don't understand their role, and they have no real clue what winning looks like. As a result, they flounder. There's hurt feelings, frustration, and a whole lot of wasted time and money. Everyone loses.

You can't just hand off a bunch of tasks and expect someone to succeed. True delegation is an investment of your time and energy and you must equip people to succeed. This means clear expectations, proper onboarding, ongoing support, and regular feedback.

Delegation Mistake #4: Not Developing Your Team Members

When you do this right, you're hiring smart, driven team players. People who are responsible, creative, and full of untapped potential. Lean into them. Don't overlook the power, benefit, and value your folks can provide. Great team members don't want to just "do their job." They want to contribute, grow, be challenged, and make an impact. If you treat them like cogs or pigeonhole them into shallow roles, you'll lose both their engagement and their full contributions.

Invite their input and ideas. Involve them in solving problems and hand over more responsibility and autonomy over time. Let them make decisions and take risks. The quicker you can tap into the power of your people, the quicker you'll see an uptick in the company culture and bottom line.

Delegation Mistake #5: Not Developing Yourself as a Leader

Don't be a boss. Be a leader. A boss relies on authority and status to get things done; a leader inspires people to move forward. Leadership isn't a destination; it's a discipline, and it never stops.

I've held all sorts of leadership positions over the years: head lifeguard, team captain, head teaching assistant, president of the skydiving club, president of a National Speakers Association chapter, and CEO. And I learned something new (and made mistakes) in every single one of them. You'll do the same, and it's part of the process. You get better over time. Stay humble enough to know you'll never "arrive" and hungry enough to keep improving. Your team deserves a great leader, and you can be that person if you commit to putting in the work.

KEY TAKEAWAYS

1. Embrace Delegation

Delegation is a non-negotiable. If you want a business that doesn't rely on you for everything, you must release control and empower others to own responsibilities. Your freedom and scalability rise and fall with your ability to delegate well.

2. Hire and Train Proactively

Don't wait until you're overwhelmed to look for help because desperation leads to bad hiring decisions. Instead, anticipate your staffing needs early, keep a steady pipeline full of potential candidates, and invest time into thoughtful onboarding and training before the need becomes urgent.

3. Have a Clear Delegation Plan

Don't wing it. A structured, well-thought-out approach to hiring, onboarding, and training ensures consistency, quality, and scalability as the business grows. Effort here is well spent and will pay huge dividends for both you and your team.

4. Use Standard Operating Procedures (SOPs)

SOPs formatted as simple, step-by-step checklists are your secret weapon for growth. They eliminate guesswork, reduce mistakes, and ensure tasks are done the same way every time, regardless of who's doing them.

5. Lean into Leadership

Your team will mirror your mindset and behavior. That means you need to set the tone for accountability, open communication, and an empowering culture. Model and support growth, encourage ownership, and foster trust. The success of your business ultimately depends on your skills as a leader.

PART VII

LIVING IT

"The best way to predict the future is to create it."

—PETER DRUCKER

CHAPTER 26:
YOUR BUSINESS FOR LIFE

As I write this, I'm overlooking the crystal-clear, aqua-blue waters of the Gulf of Mexico from a private beachfront balcony. My wife and I are on an adults-only, all-inclusive getaway, and our days have been filled with…well, pretty much nothing. We've been enjoying the sun, beach, pools, restaurants, and entertainment. It's been amazing.

What haven't I been doing? Working. I haven't spent ten minutes the entire trip even thinking about work, let alone doing any.

I'm not sharing this to brag or spark envy. I'm sharing to show you that this actually works in the real world. This isn't armchair theory. It's not hypothetical. It's practical and achievable. You can use the SEAD process in your own business just like I have in mine. And when you do, you'll enjoy the freedom that comes from having a business that doesn't come to a screeching halt without you there.

And for those of you who are thinking *"Easy for you to say,"* let me assure you—there's nothing special about me. All the credit goes to the process. Prior to applying the principles and strategies you've learned in this book, this trip would have been impossible. My business depended on me for everything. And even if by some miracle I managed to peel myself away, I wouldn't have *really* been away.

I might have been on the beach physically, but mentally I'd still be in the office. I'd feel guilty and anxious that I was on vacation instead of getting work done. I'd be staring at the ocean pretending to enjoy myself, but really, I'd just be thinking about all the tasks piling up and fires starting in my absence. And, no doubt, I would've tried to secretly sneak in some work without my wife noticing, instead of relaxing and being present.

None of that happened. I was able to completely unplug, be fully present, and enjoy the full peace of mind and confidence that comes from knowing the business was fine with me thousands of miles away. I had already done the work. I had a clear vision. I eliminated the MUD. I put smart automation in place. And I built a capable team I trusted. That's what made this trip possible.

And when I'm not on vacation, my typical workweek looks very different than it used to when I first went into business. I now work about 20 hours per week on average, and I'm focused on high-level tasks instead of putting out daily fires. My life and my business are aligned. I make it to my kids' tennis lessons, soccer practice, field trips, and doctor appointments. I hit the gym during the day. I grab relaxed afternoon lunches with my wife or friends. I take naps. I get massages. I live my life.

Maybe you're not there yet. Maybe your business would collapse if you were to take an extended trip. That's okay. Start where you are, and begin one small step at a time. You don't walk into the gym and bench press 250 pounds on day one, so don't try to change everything at once. That's a great way to crash and burn. I taught this process to a gentleman once and he got so fired up that he tried going from working 75 hours per week to 15 the very next week. The result? Picture Wile E. Coyote running off a cliff, hovering in midair, then plummeting into a cloud of smoke and a boulder landing on top for good measure.

Instead, aim for small, steady progress. If you're working 60 hours per week now, make it a goal to cut back to 55, and do it at a pace you're comfortable with. Then shoot for 50. Then 45. Even if it takes you a whole month to trim just a single hour of work per week, it adds up. In one year, you'll have reclaimed 12 hours per week. *That's a full day-and-a-half every week that you get back.* And you can always move more aggressively if you want quicker results.

As you step away, pressure-test your business to see how it holds up. Just like a plumber tests pipes for leaks, see what breaks when you're not there. Start with a half-day away. Then a full day. What happens when you're gone? Does everything run smoothly, or do things go sideways? Fix the issues, then try again. As you repeat this process with longer and longer periods of time absent, your business will become more and more stable and independent.

Each step of the process and each small improvement will create more time, clarity, and freedom. When you craft your vision in the Strategy stage, you'll have a clear picture of your priorities. Decisions get easier, distractions lose their power, and you'll enjoy a sense of confidence in your chosen direction. As you eliminate the MUD, you'll feel less overwhelmed and scattered. You'll become more streamlined and effective. When you automate, you'll be more consistent and have a solid system in place to reliably get things done. And when you delegate, you'll have a team of high-performers to help move the ball down the field while you focus on the MVPs. Each individual step of the SEAD process makes a huge difference on its own, but when you combine them all together, it becomes life-changing.

Lastly, commit to keeping the SEAD process front and center. This isn't a one-time project or a box to check. It's an operating system; a way of running your business day in and day out. As you company evolves, there will always be new distractions to eliminate, new tasks to automate, and new responsibilities to delegate. But over time, the effort required decreases as the leverage increases. Plant SEAD into your company, let it take root, and watch it grow into a Business for Life.

A CLOSING MESSAGE FROM THE AUTHOR

My fellow life-first entrepreneur,

You didn't pick up this book to learn a few new money-making tactics. You picked it up because something in your life feels off.

Maybe it's the way work seeps into everything.

Maybe it's how tired and overwhelmed you always feel.

Or maybe it's the realization that the business that was supposed to give you freedom is taking it away.

You now know the truth unless you take the time to create a clear vision, prioritize life over work, and build a business that doesn't orbit around you, freedom will always stay just out of reach.

There will be moments where progress feels slow. Times when the old way feels easier. Situations where it's tempting to jump back in and do it all yourself.

Don't.

There's too much at stake. Not just for your business, but more importantly, for your life and the people who matter most.

I don't just believe this process works, I *know* it does. I've lived it and I've seen it, more times than I can count.

SEAD doesn't just change how you run your business. It changes what your business makes possible.

Congratulations on finishing this book. What you do next is up to you, and I can't wait to see where it leads.

See you on the other side.

Yours in success,

Jason Wojo, Ph.D.

BE A HERO TO ANOTHER BUSINESS OWNER—LEAVE A REVIEW

After thousands of conversations with smart, driven entrepreneurs, I've noticed something powerful: an underlying, even if unspoken, sense of camaraderie. We understand the highs, the lows, the fears, and the joys that come with running a business that 'normal' people never will.

Along those lines, I've also noticed that the most successful owners love helping others. That's why I'm asking you for one simple favor. If you've received any value from this book, would you leave an honest review on Amazon?

It's quick, easy, costs you nothing, and could genuinely help a fellow entrepreneur who is overwhelmed, stuck, or burning out at this very moment.

To leave a review, go to **BusinessForLife.com/BFLReview** or scan the QR code below:

I realize this might appear self-serving, but let me assure you, it's not. As any author will tell you, a book sale might get you a small coffee—if you skip the oat milk.

And if you want to go full superhero mode, grab an extra copy and give it to someone who needs it. (Not *your* copy. You'll want to keep this.)

Thanks in advance, from both myself and those you're helping.

PART VIII

TOOLS AND RESOURCES

"The way to get started is to quit talking and begin doing."

—Walt Disney

BUSINESS FOR LIFE RESOURCES

Because there was no way to fit everything I wanted into this book without turning it into an encyclopedia, I created something even better: a free online resource vault.

It's chock full of valuable tools, resources, and other goodies to help you go deeper and get results more quickly as you create your own Business for Life. Inside you'll find ready-to-use checklists, assessments, plug-and-play templates, automation resources, and more.

The contents of the vault will evolve and expand over time, so check back often.

You can access it at: **BusinessForLife.com** or by scanning the QR code below:

LIFEONAIRE RESOURCES

I've mentioned Lifeonaire a few times throughout this book. I first joined Lifeonaire as a student in 2009. Years later I became a coach, then trainer, then CEO, and today I own the company.

The philosophies, strategies, and support I experienced as a member had such an impact on my life that I felt called to help others design lives and businesses that work together, not against each other.

Learn more and access free resources at: **BusinessForLife.com/Lifeonaire** or scan the QR code below:

CONNECT WITH ME ON SOCIAL MEDIA

I regularly share valuable content on business strategy, life design, freedom, mindset, SEAD, and more. If you want to keep learning and growing together, go to **BusinessForLife.com/ConnectWithWojo** or scan the QR code below:

ACKNOWLEDGEMENTS

Writing *Business for Life* has been one of the most challenging and rewarding experiences of my life. Although my name is on the cover, this book is the product of countless people who invested their time, wisdom, and encouragement along the way.

First and foremost, to God goes the glory. Here's the truth you may one day recognize: you can have all the money you want, plenty of free time, great relationships—*even abs*—and still feel like something is missing. That's because nothing in this world can fill the void that only a relationship with Jesus can.

To my book editor, Jocelyn Carbonara, my formatter Trisha Fuentes, my illustrator and friend Ben Cope, and the incredible group of beta readers, thank you for your insight, perspective, and relentless attention to detail. This book would not be what it is without your many contributions.

To Steve Cook, the founder of Lifeonaire: thank you for blazing the trail and sharing a message that has changed not only my life, but the lives of thousands. Your example, mentorship, and friendship laid the foundation for this work.

To Peter Kolat, Steve Greenbaum, and Eric Lundberg: you pushed me to grow, challenged my thinking, supported me at every turn, and believed in me when I doubted myself. You've helped me accomplish things I never could have done on my own. You're the best friends anyone could ask for.

To Angel, Ben, Paula, and other team members, past and present: you've helped me hone my leadership skills, shown me grace when I stumbled, and made it possible to live my vision. Thank you for your dedication, commitment, and friendship.

To the Lifeonaire community of members, coaches, and alumni: you are the heartbeat of this movement. Your courage to live differently, challenge conventional expectations, and design lives of meaning has been my greatest source of inspiration. This book is filled with your fingerprints.

To my family—words fall short. You mean far more to me than any amount of money, accolades, or business success. I've been deeply blessed with a loving family, both the one I grew up in and the one I'm grateful to have today. Being a girl dad (*I have three—pray for me*) is my greatest joy of all. Your voices, hugs, and laughter brighten even the darkest days.

And finally, to you, the reader: thank you for trusting me enough to pick up (and finish!) this book. My hope is that what you've read will give you not just a better business, but a better life; one filled with the riches of freedom, purpose, and fulfillment. The kind of wealth that money can't buy.